A House
and Its Atmosphere

Ben Jacks

Site Plan

1. woods road
2. stream
3. campsite
4. five-trunked oak
5. granite dome
6. swimming hole
7. stone wall
8. house
9. shed
10. garden
11. one-armed maple
12. turnaround
13. clearing
14. old foundation
15. old apple tree

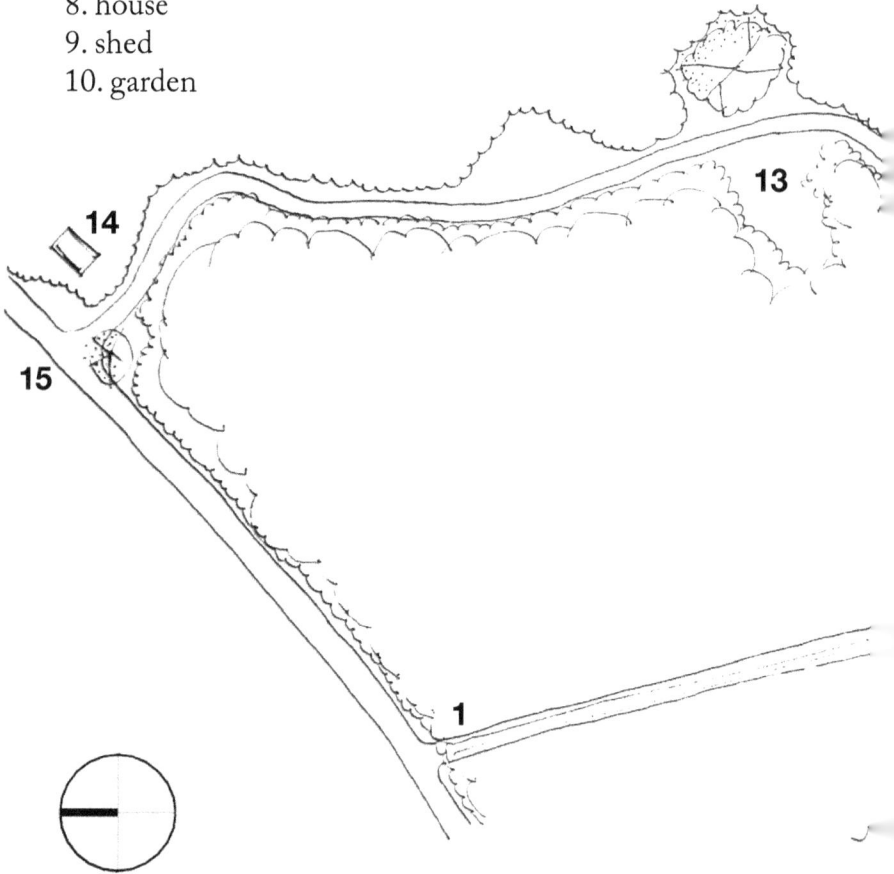

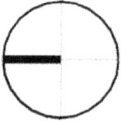

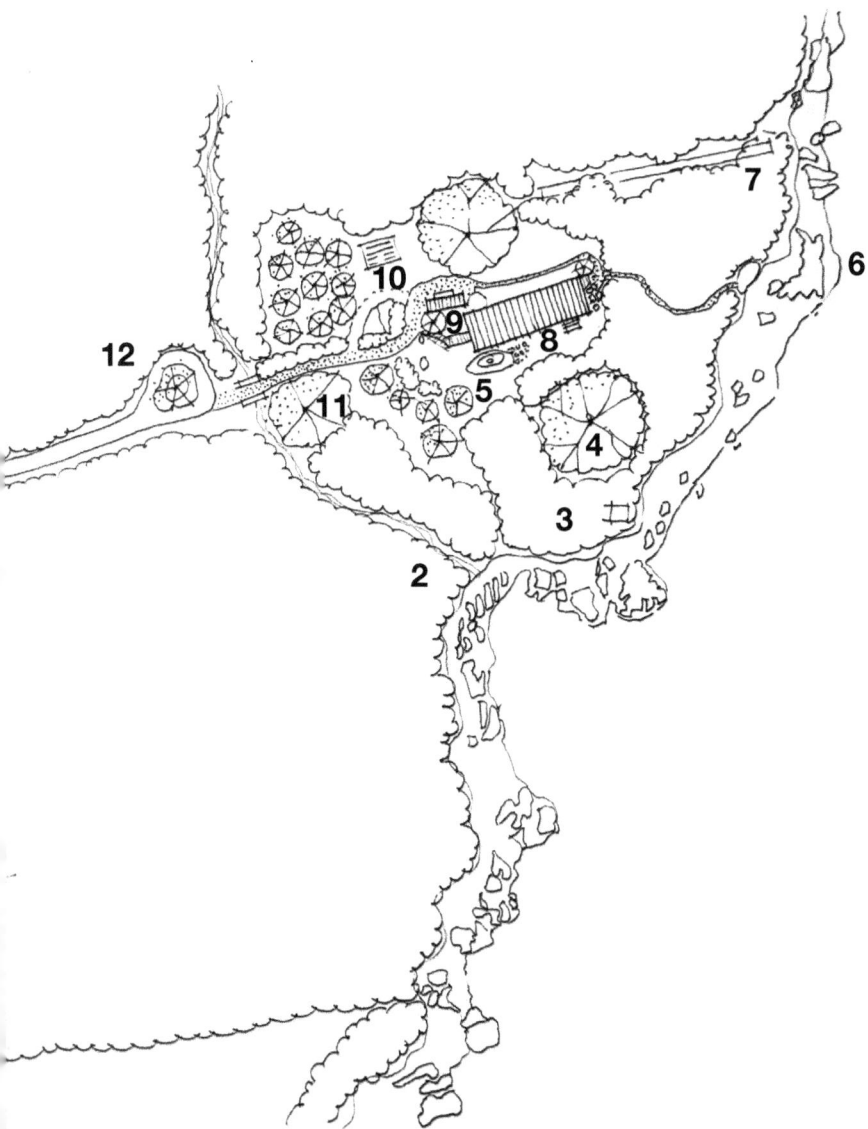

12 10 7 6 9 8 5 11 4 3 2

A House
and Its Atmosphere

Ben Jacks

Culicidae Architectural Press
an Imprint of Culicidae Press, LLC
922 5th Street
Ames, IA 50010
USA
www.culicidaearchitecturalpress.com

editor@cularchpress.com

Culicidae
Architectural Press
Ames | Gainesville | Lemgo | Rome

A HOUSE AND ITS ATMOSPHERE

For more information, please visit
www.culicidaearchitecturalpress.com

ISBN-13: 978-1-941892-24-4

ISBN-10: 1-941892-24-8

Book design by polytekton.com

for my family and friends

Table of Contents

At Pavilion House

Here in the intersection
Caught in the archway
Blown here like leaf-touch
Turned like a wind-chime
Here in the darkness
Thrown by the lightness —
Here in the shadow
Blessed by the sparkle
Here in the wooden
Sight of the moss-stone,
Here by the granite,
Here, blessing this home,

Now, the beginning,

Moved by the spruce-tips

Lupins, beginning,

Irises pointing,

Walkway beginning,

Turning past vision,

Into the shadow

Where I cannot see—

Let there be blending,

Let there be blessing,

Let there be mending,

Here, by the sea.

　　—Annie Finch
　　May 18, 2017, 2 PM

. . . trying to capture moments so they would not slip away . . .

1. Imagining

In the summer I live in a house I designed and built in the woods at the edge of a tidal cove on Deer Isle, Maine. I built the house for my immediate family, for Peggy, my wife and dearest friend for more than thirty years, and for our two children, Callie and Hugh. We first visited the island a decade ago, drawn by mere threads of suggestion, and we quickly put down strong roots. The island feels like home. But it has not always been home.

My parents lived more than a half century together—the last seventeen years in Maine—and they died together too, as often happens with lifelong partners. My father died in November of 2002, in Portland, and my mother the following May, near our home in Ohio. Because of my parents, and for many other reasons, I wanted to stay connected to Maine. Really, I wanted—impossibly—to remain connected to my parents. Grief brings its own illogic.

When we three brothers met in Portland to pour our parents' ashes into Casco Bay, I bought my first digital camera to capture the moments. I had given up film photography many years ago as a student because of the time in the darkroom and the expense. But the digital camera changed things. Camera in hand, disposing of my parents' possessions and ashes, you could say it was an attempt to look through their eyes, at their home place, in their way of seeing, or I was trying to capture moments so they would not slip away. Nostalgia is the usual derogatory term for such backward looking ancestral devotion—we Americans are eager to move on. But remembrance and its attendant nostalgia is also the way humans live on beyond a lifetime through children, and through children's children, and in that sense looking back is good and right and useful. Memory supports meaning supports memory. Identity and place attachment help people to live, too, which is the enduring value of architecture.

Peggy and I had lived in Portland years ago, when we were first married, before moving several times and eventually settling in Cincinnati, Peggy's hometown. We fondly remembered renting cottages at summer's end on two of the Casco Bay islands. Not only did we want connection to Maine for ourselves, for a larger sense of home and family, but we also wanted that connection for our children. We had learned what a slog to the start of the school year the end of summer could be, so we had resolved to go somewhere with beaches and water, a place the children might enjoy. Maine seemed a good choice, but we needed to decide exactly where in Maine. A friend mentioned Deer Isle, and the name struck a chord in me—my parents had once visited there so that my mother, a journalist who wrote about art, could interview the artist Karl Schrag. Schrag, as it turned out, had become one of my favorite artists—one of a handful of personal heroes—a bright soul in a sometimes otherwise world.

. . . a bright soul in a sometimes otherwise world . . .
Karl Schrag, "Red Sun-Dark Woods," 1991

And so it was, following intuition and breadcrumbs, that we came to rent our first house for a week of summer dwelling on Deer Isle, and we were happy there. We returned for two more years, to a different rental house the second year, enjoying the moods of light and weather, the trips to the sandy beach, and the walks in the woods. And then, in that third year, suddenly deepening our commitment to the island—to family, connection, and dwelling—we impulsively purchased the piece of land on which we would build our house.

. . . suddenly deepening our commitment . . .

. . . we impulsively purchased the land . . .

. . . it was clear the site was a good one . . .

Deer Isle, one of the larger islands in Maine, spreads out over some forty square miles, much of which is woodland. A spectacular cabled bridge, completed in 1939, connects the island to the mainland. Some 2500 people live on Deer Isle year-round, a group that swells substantially during a few weeks in summer. Fishermen, carpenters, vacationers, retirees, back-to-the-landers, organic farmers, professors, woodworkers, artists, artisans, and others intentionally populate the island. It is an unpretentious place. Home to a number of vibrant and successful cultural and community institutions, all built on passion and volunteer effort, Deer Isle was celebrated as one of seven "Imagination Intensive Communities" by the Maine Alliance for Arts Education in 2010. Especially notable are the Stonington Opera House, revitalized over the last fifteen years as a community asset, and the world renowned Haystack Mountain School of Crafts, with a campus designed by Edward Larrabee Barnes and built in 1961, winner of the American Institute of Architects' Twenty-five year Award. Working toward a common vision of what it means to dwell in a place with a strong identity, many people have staked their lives to the Deer Isle community.

Deer Isle-Sedgwick Bridge, Robinson & Steinman, 1939

Stonington Harbor

Stonington Opera House

dining hall, Haystack Mountain School of Crafts, Edward Larrabee Barnes, 1961

dining hall, Haystack Mountain School of Crafts, Edward Larrabee Barnes, 1961

gateway building, Haystack Mountain School of Crafts, Edward Larrabee Barnes, 1979

When it came time to design the house I would seek, consciously and unconsciously, to understand the relationship between ordinary design processes and practices, and theories of architecture of value to me. Phenomenology is the umbrella under which these theories generally fall. The phenomenological perspective makes two main assumptions, according to geographer David Seamon: "(1) that people and environment compose an indivisible whole; (2) that phenomenological method can be described as a 'radical empiricism.'" Seamon, who has spent a lifetime understanding phenomenological theory as the basis for environment-behavior research, elaborates:

> If one key phenomenological assumption is the intimate connectedness between person and world, a second assumption relates to what I call "radical empiricism"—the particular manner in which this person-world connectedness is to be studied. . . . In using this descriptive phrase, I attempt to encapsulize the heart of phenomenological method by indicating a way of study whereby the researcher seeks to be open to the phenomenon and to allow it to show itself in its fullness and complexity *through her own direct involvement and understanding.*[1]

But at the beginning I had no such theoretical clarity in mind because, although I had been teaching for nearly a decade, while fully immersed in ideas about architecture, I had ceased to design and actually build, and I was eager

[1] David Seamon, "Phenomenology, Place, Environment, and Architecture: A Review of the Literature," 2000. http://www.arch.ksu.edu/seamon/articles/2000_phenomenology_review.htm, (accessed January 7, 2016)

to get back to it. Designing and building the house would involve me with the land and the place; it would engage the phenomenology of making oneself at home in a strong community. It would reflect a theoretical exploration of what it means to design, to build, and to dwell. As it turned out the design process would also reaffirm that architecture arises through intuitive and non-linear thought processes, even when those processes appear from the outside to be well ordered and logical, so this book is a primary text giving access to material for a "radical empiricism" even as it attempts its own partial analysis. It combines different kinds of storytelling in the hope of revealing something about the intimacy of designing in and inhabiting a place. It is in some senses an experimental work bringing together different kinds of narratives—a diversity of parts to make a whole. It does not hew to analytical or academic forms of writing, nor is it a memoir, or an essay with photographs. It is, however, as complete and true an account as I can make of a particular episode of designing a small project and a description of the result—a house.

As it had turned out, I had become over time an on-again off-again designer and builder, a peripatetic architect who had pulled up roots several times just soon after putting them down. Pruned and trimmed, my career was sometimes cut off by forces beyond my control. When first married we settled in Portland, and I interned with good local architects, but a sharp downturn in 1990 left me unemployed even before earning a license. Then, Peggy decided to take a summer internship at the Smithsonian in Washington, a decision that prompted in me vigorous reflection about how to make the best use of my time while unemployed, which led to an exciting and ambitious plan—to hike the entire Appalachian Trail from Georgia back to Maine.

After I finished the trail, Peggy was again called to the Smithsonian, this time for a full year, and I found myself drawn into outdoor education, and a taste for teaching. From Washington we moved south, to Wilmington, North Carolina, where Peggy took her first university job, and I went into private practice. We bought our first house, an unholy wreck: a boarding house that at one time had been the Episcopal Church rectory. Restoring the building to its former glory, I began to build a practice around preservation and small projects. Our first baby, Callie, arrived in that house.

Soon Los Angeles called to Peggy: this time a year at the Huntington Library, so we made it a family adventure. As trailing spouse, I shuttered my practice while finishing a house still under construction back in Wilmington, and together we explored Los Angeles and the West. Home base was a nearly empty bungalow with lemon trees in the backyard on Las Lunas Boulevard in Pasadena. I picked up a job designing an interior renovation in San Marino, but I spent much more time tending our empty home. I remember following the racket of the feral parrots, pushing Callie in a stroller under the palm trees in Pasadena, and through the cacti and the Japanese gardens at the Huntington. Partway through the year Peggy learned of a teaching job back in Ohio and, like so many young parents, we felt called to be near family. We set up a shrine on the mantelpiece in our bungalow without furniture, and she got the job. At summer's end, we made our way back to Ohio. I began teaching, too, and loved it from the first thrilling and terrifying minute. Teaching felt like a calling. That was in September of 2000.

⧗

This book describes an age-old human process and a desire. To arrange a home around oneself is to make a place in the world. Nothing is more central to being human.

To identify place is the most important role of architecture, and the most important role of the architect is to identify place by imagining. There are, however, many ways to imagine and identify places, which vary with the geographies and cultures of people, as well as the outlook and disposition of individuals. The totality of a project, building, neighborhood, city, or other part of the built environment is involved in the identification of place and places. Identifying place through architecture is a back-and-forth process in which what is inherent in a locale begins to be taken up by building, and if building contributes to place-making, it does so in part by drawing out and drawing attention to what is already there. In place-making the whole is often greater than the sum of the parts.

The focus of the architect is not primarily on communicating a message or, what seems somehow the opposite, on solving a rational problem. When forced into one or the other of these dichotomous roles—as either an artist or as a technician—the architect easily loses sight of architecture's most important values and potentials.

Architecture is an endeavor requiring thought, but it is not primarily theoretical. Architecture's processes should result in actual space and place inhabited bodily, perceived through multiple senses.

Readers will likely recall other books in a similar vein that have come before this one, such as Charles Moore, Gerald Allen, and Donlyn Lyndon's *The Place of Houses* (1974); Tracy Kidder's *House* (1985); Witold Rybczynski's *The Most Beautiful House in the World* (1989); Ann Cline's *A Hut of One's Own* (1997); Michael Pollan's *A Place of My Own: the Education of an Amateur Builder* (1997); Bill Henderson's *Tower: Faith, Vertigo, and Amateur Construction* (2000); and Dee Williams' *The Big Tiny: a Built-it-Myself Memoir* (2015), to name a few. These books all narrate the production of a hut or house (or several houses) within a theoretical ground (explicit or implied), and also reflect on aspects of the personal experience and meaning that go along with the process of such projects, but as it turns out, these books are all different.

When I started on this building and then writing project, I imagined books like these might form a sub-genre, which I thought might be called *shelter memoir,* but I realize now that most are not actually memoir. I also believed that amateur architects or builders wrote most such books. This also turned out to be wrong. Of the seven titles above, the last three describe the work of amateurs. Add in a couple of outliers in the field, such as Eugène-Emmanuel Viollet-le-Duc's *How to Build a House: an Architectural Novelette* (1876), and Larry Haun's *A Carpenter's Life as Told by Houses* (2011), and the field tips even more sharply toward the work of professionals.

So why the assumption that there might be a sub-genre we could call shelter memoir in which someone goes into the woods to find himself by building a house? It seems revealing that Witold Rybczynski, trained as an architect, with a career as a reader-oriented writer of architectural history, theory, and criticism, concludes that the most beautiful house in the world is the one you build yourself. Perhaps most of us expect some therapeutic or redemptive value out of the accomplishment of something as large and complex as a building. Or maybe, because humans are instinctively drawn to the idea of building shelter, we expect there to be many such stories from ordinary people. Or perhaps we have such expectations because the idea of self-building is a powerful part of a narrative of self-reliance such as *Walden* and therefore it feels archetypal. Whatever the reasons for the expectation, as it turns out there are not as many shelter memoir stories as one might imagine.

The amateur-professional divide revealed in these books interests me. In *The Timeless Way of Building*, Christopher Alexander claimed, "Each one of us wants to be able to bring a building or part of a town to life like this. . . . Each one of us has, somewhere in his heart, the dream to make a living world, a universe." In a sense, all of the *Pattern Language* series was predicated on the idea that ordinary people could and should design the world around them, that if they were encouraged and supported in doing so, the world would be somehow more alive. In this view, the professionalization of design as a commercial force has led to all the dead and placeless places. On the other hand, other commercial forces operate to encourage every person to "Do-It-Yourself," with mostly abhorrent results. What could be a beautiful world, made by vernacular builders, becomes an incoherent one crammed with nonsensical products.

What is missing in the promotion of Do-It-Yourself is any level of care and concern about how design actually works. While I love a beautifully made house by an amateur—some off-the-grid hippie houses I've visited in Maine come to mind—I stand with my well-trained professionals in saying that we have some important skills to offer that take years to master. The thing is, the commercial forces impact us all; the consumer experience is marketed to amateurs and professionals alike. *Atmosphere* is anathema to commercial forces because it is also used to sell products. To discuss atmosphere seriously would be to reveal that architectural atmosphere must be created, it cannot be purchased.

My interest in this book is in describing a design process in sufficient detail to reveal the particular ways designing is an act of imagining. I want to outline the contours of this imagining, and identify some of the working parts of the process, including the moments that are unconscious or otherwise mysterious. I don't want to pretend that design processes can be cleaned up or rationalized. Rather, I want to make clear that designing is fundamentally messy, like any other creative endeavor, but that doesn't mean it can't have direction. As James Dickey put it, "A poet is someone who stands outside in the rain hoping to be struck by lightning." And so it is for designers.

*. . . out the tent door sunlight played in the leaf
litter and low hanging branches . . .*

2. Walking

A s we walk, we are in the world, finding ourselves in particular space and turning that
space by walking within it into a place, a dwelling
or territory, a local habitation with a name.

—James Hillman[2]

In 2004, I published an article in the *Journal of Architectural Education* entitled "Reimagining Walking: Four
Practices." I identified four design practices—sighting, measuring, reading, and merging— all rooted in thoughtful and
attentive walking, with the goal of articulating a process of
design that maintained the primary agency of the architect
and of architecture in the actual world. When it came time
to design my Deer Isle house I thought quite consciously of
putting the four practices to the test. Even though I identified and described the practices based on my past experience
as a design-oriented, practicing architect, this was the first
time I could apply them with conscious intention.

---

[2] James Hillman, in James Hillman, William H. Whyte, and Arthur
Erickson, *The City as Dwelling: Walking, Sitting, Shaping* (Irving, TX:
The Center for Civic Leadership, University of Dallas, 1980), p. 3

In "Reimagining Walking" I argued that sighting is "a process of walking in which the casual walker intuitively understands the relationship among physical objects in the landscape." Sighting, I theorized, "makes conscious the unconscious negotiations of landscape" through discovery of objects and landmarks, determination of alignments, and testing of possible points of view. As a design practice, sighting is fundamental to the designer's intimate understanding of the site. A simple enough conclusion—one that is right under our noses, so to speak—but all the more invisible because it is only engaged through that most quotidian activity, walking.

At first it was difficult to put theory into practice on the Deer Isle property because the land was impenetrable, at least where it mattered most, overgrown as it was with fir saplings and blocked by blowdowns. Even when we first looked at the property it was a challenge to properly see it. The real estate agent met us at a disused woods road on neighboring property and handed us maps. It was a generally flat strip 200 feet wide, nearly 1200 feet long, extending from the road to the shore in a southerly direction, with about 250 feet of frontage on a tidal cove. I knew from reading the map that if it was any good at all as a place to build a house, it would be because of the area near the cove. The agent knew this too and led us in on the woods road to the prospective building site. Near the point of crossing from the neighboring property onto the land there was a small stream surrounded by a stand of dense cattails. Once we pushed through the cattails and crossed the stream it was possible to walk the rocky shore (it was low tide). The agent showed us the first property marker at the western end of the shore frontage and then a little farther on the big ledge and boulders that would make a fine swimming hole at high tide. Then he located the farthest property marker at the end of the frontage toward the east, and we clambered up onto the bank.

Though densely overgrown, covered with blowdowns and debris, it was clear the site was a good one. It rose up from the cove gently to a piece of ledge, then sloped back down toward the small stream. The wetland areas had already been mapped, the soils tested, a road laid out, a septic system designed—all by owners who had changed their minds, given up, gotten distracted, or decided they didn't have enough money.

These were the facts, of course, but then there was our impetuous calculus, in which Peggy and I discussed, weighed pro and con, and proceeded to inevitable conclusion. We did not completely know the land—we knew it just well enough—and we bought it.

⧗

We owned the land for three years before we were ready to begin the process of design, which we hoped would soon be followed by construction. The plan was for me to camp for several days alone, to walk and measure and figure out how to position the house. Peggy, Callie, and Hugh would join me later for a week of vacation in the rental house. Then the design would be underway.

Overgrown, with no road access, threaded with a few deer paths, the prospect of systematically walking the property to understand the site seemed daunting.

Arriving late, after three hours of driving, at nearly eight in the evening, I parked the car, perching the tires on the edge of the ruts on the neighbor's woods road. Out of the car, I stepped around the deep ruts and grassy clumps, and wrote a note apologizing and explaining, sticking it under the windshield wiper. The owners might show up and the car would be in the way, and the trespassing would be obvious. I didn't want someone looking for me after dark.

The lack of an actual road suggested the neighbors used their land only occasionally. It looked like they mowed the road—really just two ruts through the grass—and mowed the clearing once a year and held a family picnic or an overnight reunion there. From a cable slung across the road between two spruce trees hung a crudely lettered sign that read "Eatons Better 'N Nuthin." It was cheerful enough—it didn't say NO TRESPASSING—but I couldn't be sure how much the cable meant "stay out," or if it was really more for stopping vehicles. I felt like I didn't belong there. Not only was I trespassing, strictly speaking, but I was also not a true islander, not even a Mainer or a Yankee, but from away—a city-slicker, a flatlander, a tourist, a summer person, whatever.

A paper parcel, there was still no way to park a car on the land. A deep drainage ditch by the side of the road was only the first obstacle and after that a thicket of forest for a thousand feet. Unlike walking on my own land, walking in on the neighbor's property was easy, first along the woods road into a grassy clearing with a plywood outhouse, and then into the margin of woods at the edge of the tidal cove. For this I felt grateful. A path, maintained mostly by deer but also probably by the occasional human, passed all along the shore and perhaps all the way around the island. Imagining the path felt like a dream: the roots and moss of it in close-up, and then the whole circumference of the island lay before me in a single compressed and translucent scene.

From the woods, stepping into the watery light at the edge of the cove, the flat felt forlorn. Low tide—the shallow cove was drained of water. The wetland stream barely trickled. This stream, and the associated wetland, had already been surveyed, inspected, and flagged by the state for protection. Orange plastic tape fluttered from a tree branch 75 feet south of the stream. Stepping from boulder to boulder, passing easily over the mud and cord grass, I reached solid ground, dropped my pack and walked out onto the farthest point of granite ledge, which was slightly elevated above the exposed mud bottom of the cove. Unlike the silk-smooth, light gray to pink granite found on most of the island, some of this granite had an unusually rough, crenellated surface that seemed volcanic in origin. A thin film of algae mixed with mud covered it below the high water line.

Measuring time with my fist there was less than one fist width, less than one hour remaining before the sun would touch the horizon, and then darkness. It's always better to be inside the tent and asleep, or close to it, when it's dark—I felt unnerved just starting to make camp so late in a strange place.

Mosquitoes approached slowly and inspected me, their prey, then moved in quickly. Swinging and slapping, to escape them I put up the tent hastily near the steel pin at the corner of the property at the edge of the cove. Parts of this process of setting up camp were second nature, so familiar from every day on the trail. Unfurl the sleeping pad, push it inside, loft the sleeping bag out of its sack, shove it in, throw in the half-full pack, crouch and scramble, pull the zipper closed, stuff a sweater into a sack for a pillow, take off blue jeans, and slide into the sleeping bag. Tired enough to skip eating, I pressed head into pillow.

But in a moment, to the horrible rising whine of a mosquito at my left ear, swatting with my left hand, I sat bolt upright. For a couple of minutes I aimed the flashlight into the corners of the tent looking for mosquitoes, snatched at three or four, and ground them into the tent fabric with familiar satisfaction.

The last of the evening light shimmered white on cream-white nylon. I lit a candle, opened a notebook, picked up a pen. Quiet at last. Enveloped in the familiar glow of the tent I leaned on one elbow into the candlelight playing on my hands and the white rectangle of paper. I breathed the dank though not unpleasant odor of camping fabric on damp earth, smelled the candle wax burning, and felt content. With the pen in my right hand I wrote the names of things I'd just left behind while walking in on the path: sun—low tide—mud—moon snail—clam flat—granite—lavender—stepping stone—driftwood. This reminded me of Wendell Berry's essay, "An Entrance to the Woods," and the sensation of leaving behind the rumble of the car and stepping onto a path in the woods, where some sweetness of light and air descends and a "lonesome melancholy" permeates everything, only my list was long, the rupture not so sudden or certain as Berry's. And continuing: pipe stem—cove—clear sky—trail—oak branch—club moss—fern—deer scat—plastic—spruce—outhouse—stone wall—sign—steel cable—lichen—kayak—farmhouse—car. I felt excited. At last I was beginning. Buildings, like poems, begin with the naming of things.

Eyes closing, I blew out the candle, slid down into the sleeping bag, and drifted into sleep. Soon I was startled awake to branches snapping, hurried stamping, hooves on packed earth, clattering on stones down the bank of the cove, then the warning snort-whistle of deer. Where the noise was coming from I couldn't tell exactly, or how many animals there were—only that they were trotting and bounding away. Camped in the deer path I must have upset the nightly passage. You'd think I'd be no longer afraid of such doings-after-dark, but I was. When I hiked the Appalachian Trail for half a year I slept almost every night in a tent. Sometimes I awoke to silence, or footfall, or scuffling among leaves, or the *pree-tee-prank* of raindrops sloughed suddenly off a sheaf of leaves. Or I'd awake not having slept, in the ordinary sense, rather having spent the night turning, tensing, bracing against cold or a particular discomfort: a root, a rock, hard ground, or clammy moisture. Sometimes I'd awaken terrified in the middle of the night and listen to unplaceable sounds: wild boar digging roots, or a rabbit screaming moments before being torn to shreds, or I'd awaken suddenly from a nothingness so profound that waking up felt urgent.

⧗

Dogs barking and men shouting. Motionless and rigid, I listened and breathed slowly, straining to hear, terrified. The noises stopped, and then started up again. Were the men moving, or remaining in one place, or headed my way? Or maybe no one would be interested in a tent at the edge of a cove on an anonymous shore.

⧗

Some large hollow-sounding object, perhaps a plastic or wood boat, scraped across shells and mud and I awoke. It was still dark but near dawn. Though I did not hear speech I soon decided there were two men. First I unzipped the tent door and then the fly. The stones exposed along the edge of the cove shone white. It was low tide again: high tide had come and gone in the night. I felt alone.

The thwack and scrape of tools in mud began. The men were digging clams. A practiced, slightly mournful, regular rhythm, broken from time to time by a dull thud and dragging, it felt as if it emanated from the land and water itself. I loved listening. It sounded like we humans belonged, and we were at home.

⧖

The tent in full glow—morning at last—I rolled over, sat up, unzipped the door and the fly and secured it. Out the tent door sunlight played in the leaf litter and low hanging branches. Time to get up, I crawled out the tent door.

From the campsite by the steel pin the land sloped up through the woods. Up past a mature oak tree with five trunks, past a large boulder beneath a scraggy conifer skeleton, I walked to where the woods opened to what looked like the end of an old farm road. Smooth pink granite ledge pushed up in two great domes at the highest point and beside the largest of these domes was a heap of fieldstones. No doubt the fieldstones were moved here a few at a time until the fields were let go about 1940. Before that most of the island was open for sheep pasture, orchards, and gardens. I was excited to think I could walk the path from here to the campsite on the shore every day when the house was built. Deciding to set up here to think about the house, I went back for the camp chair, stove, cook pot, coffee cup, food sack, water jug, drawing and measuring tools, and the Japanese saw.

. . . past the large boulder beneath the scraggy conifer skeleton . . .

But where and how to build the house, precisely? Standing there, survey in hand, looking to the north in the general direction of the road a thousand feet away, I couldn't move more than a few yards. Spruce trunks, each more than twelve inches in diameter, lay across one another in a tangle. The trees, a dozen or more, fully mature, had fallen in winter, perhaps in a nor'easter. Most simply snapped a few feet above the ground, some broke into several pieces, and one, perhaps stronger than the rest but caught by the domino effect, overturned completely, its roots pulled up in a great earthen wheel of moist soil.

Beyond the tangle of tree trunks, not far past a mature maple tree, lay the stream and wetland. A heavy limb extended out from the tree trunk at nearly a right angle then pointed straight up like a human arm. To understand the shape and slope of the land, to fit the house gently, to design with the land, to shape the approach to the house so it arcs and unfolds, I needed to get through to that maple. Maybe there was an easier way to the maple, a path of least resistance, or a way around the inevitable struggle over, under, and through the spruce trunks.

But first, coffee. Turning back to the granite ledge, the camp chair dropped on the highest point, I settled into it, positioned the stove, pumped it twenty-five times, lit it, pumped some more, poured water, set the pan on the stove, got out the coffee and set it up and settled back. It was a routine from the trail. In minutes the water would be boiling and poured and the coffee would be nearly ready. The sun was off to the east through dense, dark trees, out toward ever widening water and eventually the Atlantic Ocean. Sitting there all day—I wasn't going to because I had work to do—the sun would rise from the water and in late morning it would begin to light the open space and arc to about 75 degrees above the horizon then, in the afternoon, it would descend behind me all afternoon, sending warming rays.

The house should take advantage of the sun's path—this should be a first concern of the architect. The house ought to start there near the rising granite and stretch out long and narrow toward the south, or bend to shape some outdoor space, or break into two or more pieces, aware of the sun. Perhaps it could fold to form a courtyard, or a half-courtyard, or an outdoor half-room. All of these ideas about the house were vivid—complete and pure potential—and it felt wonderful and exhilarating to think of them, but I'd have to choose, and that was a frightening prospect. For the time being I was free to imagine anything: walls of glass and dusty metal, a reflecting pool, a building formed among boulders, a weaving among trees, a house unfolding toward the sky like a river.

A teacher of mine had once explained how the great Finnish architect Alvar Aalto approached design. He preferred to stay in the fantasy rather than go too quickly into the hard reality demanded by drawing the building. He spoke of the dream that would shatter the moment the pencil hit paper. He too made coffee to delay the disruption of the imagined sense of things by the hard reality of facts.

Water boiled, rattled the pot lid. Steam rose. The stove shut down, water dribbled and bubbled over fine black coffee grounds. Then, pouring faster, the coffee water plinked in the bottom of the cup.

The next move was to measure or, as I had theorized, begin the process of "walking to determine the dimensions of land and relative locations of objects." Ideally, the task was to survey, measure, and commit the site to bodily memory. Instead, a good part of the morning was spent sipping coffee, which was a pleasure. When I stood at last on the Western property line trying to understand it I felt confused about how to begin the actual practice of measuring. With a pencil stuck behind my ear, and a copy of the survey in hand, I walked back and forth along the line several times counting paces from the camp at the steel pin to the point along the line where the forest opened up toward the east into the impenetrable blowdown. The line didn't make sense, even though surveyors had cut along it through the woods repeatedly over the years—there were stumps and more recent slash cuts to prove it. Every once in a while there was a piece of orange plastic surveyor's tape, but the line seemed to cut back toward the road at far too steep an angle. Although this was perhaps only an illusion of disorientation that would diminish over time, the chaos of woods and ground confounded what was on the page. The western property line didn't seem to relate to the high point of land where it seemed likely the house would want to go.

When I hiked the trail I spent a lot of time in forests, following white blazes from Georgia to Maine, making measurable progress every day, always moving on, never lost, but here I felt stopped and stuck. Nothing seemed to add up in the tangle of trees and undergrowth. I felt bewildered—as in wilderness—disconnected, aimless, and without movement. Time seemed hard to track, hard to follow.

⌛

The rounded slap of water at the granite ledge in the cove meant it must be near high tide, or just after.

Perhaps there could be a different approach to disorientation: forget the property line for a while and see if it would be possible to make it through to the point near the stream where the final approach to the house might begin. Thinking about planning the site for a while on paper, it had made sense to stop the road on the other side of the stream and create a long pedestrian path from there, perhaps with a bridge over the stream. But first, to get to where the imagined bridge would be, it would be necessary to climb through the blowdown, or walk around it. Uncertain about the danger, I felt unsure exactly how to climb through or around the blowdown safely.

Stepping up on a limbless spruce trunk, I inched along, balanced as on a tightrope. Fir and spruce seedlings had already started up next to the trunks in furious clumps, fueled by the sun over the new opening in the forest. Ground plants thrived there too—wild raspberries and grasses mostly, but also some club mosses and ferns in the shadows of the trunks. A few young conifers, several feet tall, were full and dark green, bounding up, unlike the wispy trees started and forced to grow under the canopy.

Stepping down off the trunk, stopping to examine the enormous disk of upturned roots and soil, the exposed soil offered a kind of effortless archeological dig in a layer from the past that isn't normally visible. It was studded with small pieces of broken rock and larger rounded glacial stones, but one shape stood out, for it was nearly square. Breaking it from the hard soil, cleaning it off with spit, it looked like a clay potsherd. It was light red and porous, striated the way a pot might be, but it was also a perfectly ordinary pale color, lacking any decoration or sign of firing. Native people used the cove as a protected canoe route, and this particular place seemed as good as any for camping on the side of what was known as "Indian Carrying Place." Traveling by canoe indigenous people would have likely found it desirable to wait until high tide in order to paddle effortlessly through from the east side of the island to the west. The fragment was a trace of centuries of camping.

Back on the spruce trunk, an elevated spot within the blowdown, the one-armed maple was a likely point of origin for the approach path to the house. Such landmarks were beginning to take on identity—parts of the land were beginning to have names. Just beyond the one-armed maple ferns and other large-leafed wetland plants grew in profusion. From there I might be able to run the line to the high point of granite ledge where the house would begin, which would reveal both the approach through the blowdown and the slope of the topography. I walked as far as I could on the spruce trunk until limbs obstructed the way. The limbs were rock hard, full of crystallized resin, but they broke easily out of the trunk, which felt soft, maybe even rotten. The trunk cut easily with the Japanese saw even though it was more than a foot in diameter. It might be possible to cut a path through the blowdown even without a chainsaw, though at the moment that was far from sure.

Back to the spot on the granite ledge in full sun, I drank water, ate a banana, and made more coffee. Warmed and comfortably seated, studying the shape of the opening the trees made to the sky, I examined the trees in the surrounding forest. There were some really healthy ones up there, in contrast to the fallen trees a little farther down slope toward the wetland where there was so much a sense of death. There was an enormous spruce there, a white birch, and a magnificent oak, all of which were half-concealed, crowded in by lesser trees. They could be opened up from within the forest by careful thinning. Tending the forest would be a bit like gardening, with all of gardening's spiritual reward.

There was an area the shape of a saddle stretched between the highest dome and another smaller piece of the granite ledge, but it was covered with a couple of dozen dead or nearly dead fir trees all still standing. It seemed like it might be a natural threshold, a good place from which to enter the house. Kneeling in the duff I cut away a few of the lowest branches of one tree then cut through the base of the trunk, which cut easily. The tree began a slow fall, but stopped, its dry, stiff branches deeply interlaced with the branches of other trees surrounding it. Grabbing the butt of the trunk, dragging it several feet away, the tree fell, then I stripped it of branches, then cut down a dozen more and dragged them out of the way too. Now it was possible to see through to the clearing.

Through the woods to the east there were some trees down and others leaning. The earth was damp and soft—though thinking this I was reaching past the simpler explanation for why the trees fell: they had reached the end of their lives. Although I did not know it then, I know now that after a certain age, perhaps six or seven decades, if not sooner, they succumb quickly to heart rot, which weakens the core of the tree and is sometimes accompanied by a telltale shelf fungus on the trunk, and then they die by snapping off at the trunk—sometimes in calm weather without warning.

⌛

Through all the looking and slow moving over and through the trees and around the dome there was one firm conclusion: the floor level of the house, especially at the point of entry, should be lower than the dome of granite. When you entered the house you should have the sense that, although the house was built at a high point of land, it was not built at the highest point. Or at least in the relationship between the house and this natural threshold, the house should be subordinate to the dome of granite—the earth should win. To think of topography this way is to say that even in shaping a place we are only guests and our tenure is temporary. In this decision, even though it did not yet reveal a larger vision for the house, it was thrilling to recognize a truth.

⧖

Up again, back to the task, picking through the woods around upturned roots and over sap-sticky trunks and through tangled sticks toward the one-armed maple, which was now a familiar marker, I tied the yellow nylon line to a broken limb and pushed it up against the tree so the line was held high. Reversing direction and following along the line, I climbed back through the blowdown tangle again, stretched the line to the saddle-shaped threshold, drove a stake into the ground, tied the line to it, and pulled the yellow line tight, describing a level datum over a distance of 150 feet. The grade change over the approach path was about nine feet overall, much more than it appeared to be. As a numerical abstraction nine feet was difficult to understand, but having gone through the process of measuring by clambering under and over and through the blowdowns the shape and feel of the topography began to be clear.

Following the straight path of the yellow nylon line I began to cut. The curved saw sliced easily through the punky tree trunks. Sections of trunk a foot in diameter and several feet long dropped to the ground and rolled easily out of the way. It was exhilarating to cut and create a perfectly clear straight path along the yellow line.

Placing one foot in front of the other I went slowly. Walking through leaf litter, kicking sticks and fragments of bark out of the way, I cleared the path. Walking slowly down the grade toward the one-armed maple, around stones and clumps of ferns, following as straight a line as possible, then reversing and walking up the slight slope from the one-armed maple to the saddle-threshold next to the granite dome, I returned to the place where the house would start. Standing on the saddle-threshold in full sun, looking down the line into the forest, the one-armed maple was in deep shade, almost as far as the wetland around the stream. In the clearing the ground was dry and full of dried straws and sticks. Walking back again out of the sun into the cool of the forest, where the ground was damp and green, covered in ferns and club mosses, I stood on the roots of the one-armed maple and looked back up the line to the saddle-threshold. It felt like success. Walking the new path over and over in a pilgrimage against bewilderment, following the yellow string, I began to know in my body the way the grade changed and how the yellow line related to the once confusing western property boundary. There were now familiar landmarks, provisional, temporary, and permanent: the One-Armed Maple, the Granite Dome, the Saddle-Threshold, and the Start-of-House.

⧗

Late afternoon. Back on top of the granite dome, the stove hissed and chugged like a toy train, boiling water for noodles. Back pressed into my camp chair, legs tired and knees sore, notebook in lap, I sketched blocks of space in black ink, translating the blocks into views of windows and walls wedged between trees. A series of blocks, linked, extended the house toward the cove to the south, forming a long western wall. Imagination played dappled light across weathered shingles, felt the wall's mass, weight, density, texture, height, scale, and proportion. Only a little of this made it onto the page—it was all vision, short on actual detail—but it was a start.

The sun was beginning to color everything with an orange light. The air was shifting to evening air. Diagramming was simple arithmetic that didn't capture the effects of light: multiplying and adding, conjecturing about feet and modules in one sketch, height and proportion in another, an idea about a large roof overhang in another. After the long approach from the one-armed maple, the house would begin in actual space, in a half-room on the saddle-threshold, in a place to arrive before entering. Other than that, I didn't know very much.

Architectural design is above all an imaginative process. In this it is related to memory. The designer imagines an entire environment that does not yet exist. The designer starts from nothing, or from some actual place that will be transformed. Daydreaming design, if it begins or will end in an actual place, will need to be tempered by geometry, measure, and proportion. This is where sighting and measuring come in: with a full bodily understanding of how things line up, and how they relate to one another on terrain and in space, the designer may work with an actual situation, rather than with an abstract and ungrounded one. Sighting and measuring as conscious practices bring precision and accuracy to a designer's imaginings. Tools such as scaled plans and computer models help in this process—they are essential to communication and coordination of intent—but they also can mislead the designer, keep him removed from actual space and place and if misused mislead to placelessness and inhuman built environments. By walking, map in hand, the thought on paper can be properly united to mind. The mind, as neuroscientists have demonstrated, is not a separate sphere from the body. Mind and body move together in atmosphere.

Building deep knowledge, walking the path from the one-armed maple to the saddle-threshold, the abstraction of nine feet of grade change over 50 yards became specific through sighting and measuring. Sighting and measuring, using specific tools to do so, I was also reading and merging; the walking practices of design are never fully separate from one another. Together they are more like thinking with the body and the mind at the same time—one moment slipping into the atmosphere of the place, the next picking out its disparate and constituent parts, then pacing and counting, then seeing what lines up with what—then doing it all again, up and down the scales in practiced knowing.

In architecture, the passage from one place to the next, the threshold, is everything, and it serves many purposes. Make a roof on a house that works like the space beneath the fly on a tent—good for keeping things dry, and good for making transitions—and you may make a roof that flies, or flaps its wings, that in its form acknowledges the gently bending tops of trees. Or make a room with a diaphanous quality, that is all threshold and transition that opens up like a pavilion in the forest. Marco Frascari used to say, in his lovely, bouncing Italian-accented English, "Architects are lika fortune tellers—they predicta the future." That is what I was playing with—predicting the future.

On the Appalachian Trail each day started with a plan, the general contours of which were roughly the same: drink water, slide up and out of the sleeping bag, out through the zippers, walk away to pee, return to camp. Boil water for coffee, settle back to rest for a while, write notes about the previous day's events, or perhaps open the tent door enough to watch morning arrive. Sip coffee and wait to feel moved to get up again, to get serious about breakfast, about arranging, packing, planning, and going. On that path every morning, hardly having to think of which way to go, it practically pulled me forward, which was both reassuring and conducive to long meditation. Camping here, however, forced to go slow, to stay, to look, to wait, to listen to the sounds of the air, land and water, to know where the deer paths went, what the mosses looked like, where the magnificent trees stood, where the light would lay next, how the air would shift direction, how the tide rose and fell, I was beginning to know the place.

Steam rattled the lid of the cookpot and billowed, water boiled over and sizzled. Lifting the lid, I broke dry noodles into the pot, stirred them, let them simmer, and after a while took the pot off the stove. A day's work over, I sat for a while, eating and drinking, felt the sun slip down behind the trees. The air turned distinctly cool, then shifted direction.

Soon it would be time to head back to the tent. The shadows appeared deep and indistinct and the woods lacked color. After picking up the camp tools and surveying tools I walked down through the woods, past the big boulder on the left, the wild, bare-branched spruce, the five-trunked oak. At the tent I dropped my things under the tent fly, walked a few yards up the western property line just to have another look, and returned. In the morning I'd have to start again to understand the measure and orientation of the boundary line. I brushed my teeth, drank some water, and walked out of the tree line onto the granite ledge rising out of the mud in the cove. The tide was dead low. It would rise in the night and be low again by morning.

It would take a couple of days, but by spending time on the land, the landmarks would last and be known—the granite dome, the five trunked oak, the one armed maple, the silvered skeleton of half of an ancient spruce, the swimming ledge at the shore. These elements would help organize the site and the house—they were already beginning to do so.

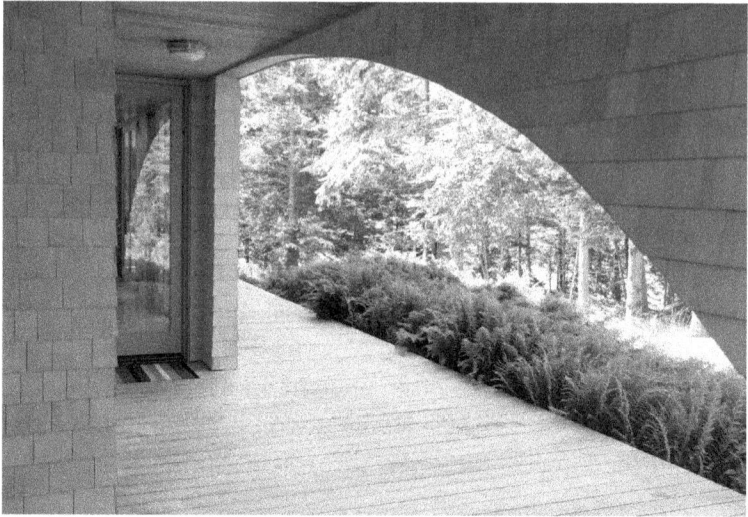

"... *whatever the human proposes and makes becomes a life* ..."

3. Designing

The room is the beginning of architecture. It is the place of mind. You in the room with its dimensions, its structure, its light responds to its character, its spiritual aura, recognizing that whatever the human proposes and makes becomes a life.

—Louis I. Kahn[3]

Cultural, geographical, physical, and sensual understandings of place are at the root of the design of any good house. The design process involves both abstract work and actual work on a site while walking and imagining. A design, like place identification itself, involves multiple layers of interpretation and understanding.

As a foundational theorist of phenomenology in architecture, Christian Norberg-Schulz pursues the idea of a

---

[3] Louis I. Kahn, "The Room, the Street, and Human Agreement," talk given on the occasion of the awarding of the Gold Medal of the American Institute of Architects, 1971.

requisite "existential foothold," a synonym for Heidegger's "dwelling," and a pre-requisite for place identification. In *Existence, Space, and Architecture*, Norberg-Schulz distinguishes five distinct space concepts: (1) the pragmatic/physical space of animal instinct; (2) the space of perception, orientation, and identification; (3) existential space, which gathers into stable images of the world; (4) cognitive space, in which humans are able to think about the physical world; and (5) the abstract space of pure logical relations such as mathematics.

Within this nested hierarchy of conceptualizations of space, the human perceives, participates in a social/cultural totality, and engages the possibility of being able to build, think about, and make architecture. All of these concepts point to aspects of the human need to know how and where one exists, a need that architecture holds out the promise of fulfilling. The fulfillment of this need begins with the identification of place and extends to the more elaborate manifestations of dwelling.

Norberg-Schulz's five nested space concepts, particularly the lower order ones, provide a useful framework for experience on the land. First of all, the most animal of human space concepts, what Norberg-Schulz calls *pragmatic space,* dominated my experience of camping on the land, which required first crawling, then cutting through downed trees and tangles of brush, before walking more or less freely became possible. This lengthy process of discovery preceded any genuine prospect of decision or design. Second, the topography and ecology of the site began to be revealed while walking: the perception of gravity (the forest's materiality and the ground's slopes, both perceived through the feet), vision (views, alignments, the forest's open-closed, inside-outside nature), and the other senses (smell, touch, hearing, vision, temperature). It would be a conventional statement, but also a mistake to say that nothing was there on the land: stands of barren, short-lived fir trapped among venerable red oaks and towering spruce; a stream separated the tip of the point from the rest of the land; a dome of granite rose out of the highest point. It would be no exaggeration to say that the design began using things that were there: that dome above all, among boulders and big trees.

Once the design had begun to arise, through suggestions of topography, the concept of "existential space," entered in. That is, architecture's history, both narrow and broad—in Maine's vernacular, ways of building, local culture, how the place is situated and imagined, etc. Fourth and finally, fifth, the design came filtered through cognition of the physical world, opinions about it, and through rational and mathematical thinking about space, use, measure, proportion, materials, budget, and so on. In other words, there is a phenomenology of process as well as a phenomenology of architecture. From within the alchemy of process springs the unconscious source.

. . . a dialogue to entertain between the Maine vernacular . . .

... and Modern stylistic idiom as propagated
by Barnes' Haystack ...
studio block, Haystack Mountain School of
Crafts, Edward Larrabee Barnes, 1961

After sighting and measuring, the next practices in my theory of walking for design are reading and merging. Reading has to do with identifying, drawing out, and creating the layered narratives of meaning that would inform the design and experience of the house. There are a number of significant design precedents on Deer Isle to consider and perhaps allude to or acknowledge: above all, the vernacular unique to Maine, to the coast, and even to Deer Isle, but also the Haystack campus five miles down the road, which is a significant part of the Deer Isle legacy because of the artists and craftspeople the school has attracted to settle on the island, which in itself pays homage to vernacular ways of building. There is a dialogue to entertain between the Maine vernacular and Modern stylistic idioms, as propagated by Barnes' Haystack. Material choices and formal arrangements might allow for straightforward and substantial construction that would last a long time with minimal maintenance and excellent performance in the maritime climate, not only as a practical matter, but also as an understanding about coastal building traditions. The existing buildings are texts within context and they may be read for pleasure, consciously and unconsciously, and for the dialogue among them, as with books on a shelf.

Reading, as a practice of design, has to do with the intersection of cultural texts, ideas one has entertained over time, personal experience, and actual space and place, all of which exist along a continuum. If the built environment is to work, it must allow the individual to feel these diverse aspects of experience, to feel that they are at least connected to one another, if not fully integrated. Reading has an aspect that may be communicated in words, or in specific visual images that may be talked about, but reading is also experiential and has to do with scale.

⧖

I arrived at the idea of a long, narrow building in a couple of stages. First, the speculative, imagining phase that began the moment we bought the land and then, much later, understanding the land and testing the idea. Peggy and I had developed the design while staying in a rental house overlooking a well-traveled waterway out of Stonington Harbor. We sat on the broad porch of the turn-of-the century foursquare in the evenings sipping wine while the kids played hide and seek at the edge of the forest. We talked and sketched and made notes while sailboats and lobster boats came and went. The air, lifted up onto the porch from the warm slope that extended down to the water, moved in response to the slightest movements of the ocean, and it made so much sense to be staking a good piece of our lives—many summers going into the future—to this island.

In some ways the process of deciding on space require-ments had been mechanical and simple. Frustratingly, there was very little to deciding on spaces and functions. It was a short list on paper that seemed to move us only insignifi-cantly closer to designing, building, or finishing the house, but it was nevertheless a beginning: we had to start some-where. We knew we wanted a bunkroom. We wanted it to be possible for lots of children to be able to come and visit, and we wanted the house to have actual beds for family (we counted fourteen), even while keeping the house modest. We also knew, from the house we were renting and those we had rented in the past that it made sense to put a bathroom on each floor, accessible by anyone in the house. In rental houses we usually relinquished the upstairs bathroom to children and used the downstairs bathroom ourselves. This was how vacation life worked—some days you didn't even shower. Be-yond that we would need a mudroom and then one enor-mous space for cooking, eating, and being together. That was the list: nearly complete and wholly inadequate, but carefully and neatly written down on a piece of lined paper.

It was pleasurable to think about the non-existent future house when we were on the island, but it became much harder far away in Cincinnati, while overwhelmed by the dailiness of school and work. We'd be in the car on our way somewhere and one of us would start to say something and we'd be off describing, imagining, and restating our conclusions about the kinds of rooms and spaces we wanted and needed—bunk-room, kitchen, mudroom, bath. We went over the same list and the same ideas again and again. During this phase Peg-gy sometimes wanted to start saying particular things about the design of the house but it seemed better to change the subject, to prevent speaking in specific terms and return again and again to, "What do we need? What kinds of rooms do we want?" It would be better to design the building by avoiding preconceptions, neither remaining stuck in thinking about functional requirements nor chasing after form.

How might the building or rooms fit best on the site within the setback lines and take best advantage of the site's potential without ruining it? The building could not evolve as an abstraction without concrete reference to the facts of soil and stone. How would the rooms stack up in certain combinations, one above the other, this adjacent to that? Each space and room faced particular restrictions: each needed a door of a certain kind, a window, and an orientation, or complete reinventions of these conventional things. Peggy and I sat together at the kitchen table, and I listened patiently as she picked up the pen and a scrap of paper, began to draw, and made authoritative declarations such as, "The only way it makes sense is to lay out the second floor like this . . . ." Her drawings involved rectangles without right angles, and bold declarations about dimensions that didn't add up, but long ago I learned to shut up and listen.

⌛

After preliminary efforts over a long period of time in various settings—on the site, and then back home in Cincinnati, in the car and at the kitchen table—one day in late spring I began to scratch away alone at pieces of paper, this time in earnest commitment to a complete set of drawings meant for construction.

I set up a drafting table in the sunroom at the east end of our house. The sunroom used to be a porch with two Doric columns set between two stuccoed corner piers, but the previous owner enclosed the porch, somewhat clumsily, with casement windows and a French door. We have always called the room "the couch room," because it barely contains a ten-foot long Italian sofa covered in rust red linen, but only now does it occur to me that the couch may be a metaphoric one. "Wallace," a sculpture by the artist William King, given by my father to my mother when they were first engaged in the fifties, stood in the corner. "Wallace" reminded me of my father in his stance and gait. Overhead, along the wide frieze board that crowned the couch room, were fifteen carved wood puppet heads from Indonesia sold to my parents in the fifties as early American folk art, an unscrupulous and common practice at the time. There was Punch and Judy, the devil, the monk with a heart painted on the top of his head, the African, the before and after bloody-faced man, and a Hitler look alike (which, if it were so, would belie origins before the 1930s). There was also a wall of books, including my godmother Siasia's books from her friend Lewis Mumford and, to the left of the books, four paintings: all color variations on a single composition of a southern hound dog by an artist from Wilmington, North Carolina where we once lived—the "dogues," we call them, in a sort of swampland brogue. The room used to look out from under the shade of a massive red oak, down the slope into a ravine toward the Cincinnati zoo, that is, until we had to take the old tree out, a victim of all manner of fungus. But before then, when I began drawing with many ancestral eyes looking over my shoulders, the ancient oak was resplendent with foliage that shimmered in the spring light, throwing its elliptical shadows across the grass.

Beginning with conviction, firm in the idea of a long and narrow house, confident of the location of the house on the site after my camping excursion and walking experiments, I began to trace over the site maps, to spin out arrangements of rectangles, and to otherwise make a mess of the drafting table.

After a while I carried curled sheets of yellow trace from the room and laid them before Peggy as questions and evidence of progress, sometimes interrupting her tea and reading. She was the ideal client: we debated particular points, talked over conceptions, misconceptions, and perceived restrictions. After a while—hours and days—uncertainty was lifting. Decisions were made, or tested anyway, and in this way over the course of a week a reasonably solid idea of how the building might be arranged eventually arrived. Following the rule that simplicity would govern when possible, I would always choose the simpler of two alternatives.

Upstairs there would be a long hall on the east side of the building. Along the hall, on the right, would be our bedroom, then the bathroom, two bunkrooms for children. At the end of the hall would be the largest room, a library and a guest room in one—since it would be at the end it would have the best view toward the cove to the south. At the north end of the long hall, the stairs down would open into a mudroom with another bathroom and the mechanical spaces off of it. The mudroom would open, next to the front door, into the main part of the house: the interconnected kitchen, dining room, and main living room. Since the topography sloped slightly to the south from the granite dome, the floor level changed to follow the grade. Large doors would let us out into the landscape in intimate contact with the forest and the rising and falling tide. To accommodate all of this it made sense to use a series of six modules, each twelve by sixteen feet, within which the required spaces fit together on the proper floors. These modules were also laid out in the drawings, at least in approximate terms, and they began to give the plan some organizing geometry and proportion.

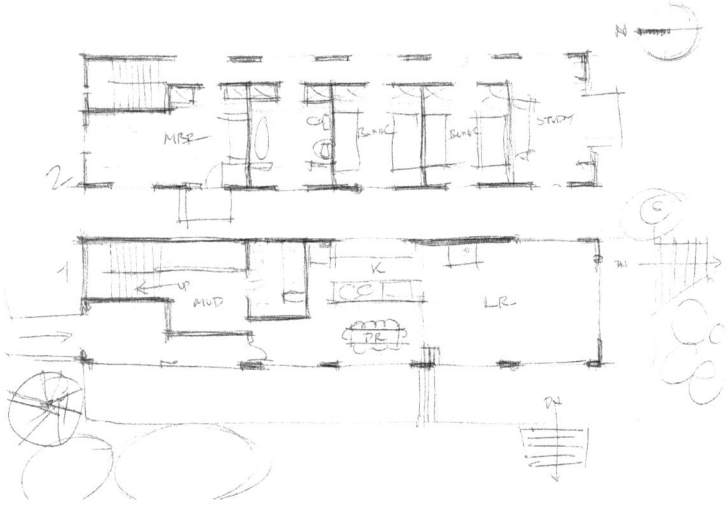

. . . it sounds and looks as if designing was easy and direct . . .

It sounds, and looks, from a late-in-the-process sketch, as if designing was easy and direct, but there were many now forgotten days of seemingly aimless and tiring work, followed by sleepless nights, staring at the ceiling and its rectangular moons. There were trips for cups of coffee. As in stories it's not in the dramatic moments where the work gets done. After drawing and redrawing the house dozens of times in plan, section, and elevation, it was at last pleasing in dimension, measure, and proportion.

It was also late spring—time to send the construction drawings off to Todd Lawson, the contractor in Deer Isle. In just a couple of months we would return to Deer Isle for two weeks in a rental house. If all went well, Todd would tell us what the house would cost, and we would begin.

One of the challenges of designing something is dealing with the recognition that the thing designed is but one possible thing of an infinite number of possibilities. It is an illusion to believe that the house designed is inevitable, though it needs to feel that way. A theoretical framework or a notion does not lead to a neat result. Rather, designing is part of the process of radical empiricism that is as messy as life itself.

⌛

The identification of place distinguishes architecture from all other arts. Further, such identification of place is specific—places contain what Simon Unwin helpfully calls "frames of reference for doing." My house would have no single frame of reference or single center, but rather a number of frames that would interact with and overlap one another within the whole. Places for "sitting while socializing"—the dining table, the living room, the kitchen, the hearth—all would claim the place of "heart" or center of the house, depending upon the activity of users.

What would stand between these centers along the lines separating them and marking a significant shift in floor level? What objects and materials would help define where one room, defined by use, gives way to another in otherwise unified space? "Social geometry" centers each such act of dwelling, and places each act in tension with the "ideal geometry" of squares and 1:2, 2:3, and golden mean rectangles. To what extent are such potentially competing geometries explicit and defined?

As aspects of the actual built space, light and ventilation would be even more significant actors than geometries. The main room, situated at the end of the building, positioned as on a point, would open on three sides to the forest and the water's edge, which is sensed and seen in glimpses. The monumental glass walls—ten feet by ten feet—could be opened and closed in response to shifting weather. Rain, fog, cold-damp air, warm-dry air, salt-air, pine-scent, sunlight, breezes from every direction—the most significant phenomena of life in the maritime forest at the ocean's edge—might place into tension the idealized space of the room. Sensational phenomena, what Unwin calls architecture's *modifying elements*, would combine with the far more constant but still changing daily transit of the sun. Stasis, by contrast, makes evident the dynamic phenomena that move around and through the room. In Unwin's method of analysis natural phenomena can organize the experience of a space.

To reflect on the origin of a design that strongly privileges aspects of architecture such as light, sound, touch, color, texture, temperature, smell, ventilation, and time, is to pursue what Juhani Pallasmaa values as "deeper unconscious intentions." Such intentions harken back to childhood experience where, in the sanctity of light on a summer afternoon in a beautiful room in the old farmhouse where we lived, I was at once aware of a presence in a moment, and I felt fully alive.

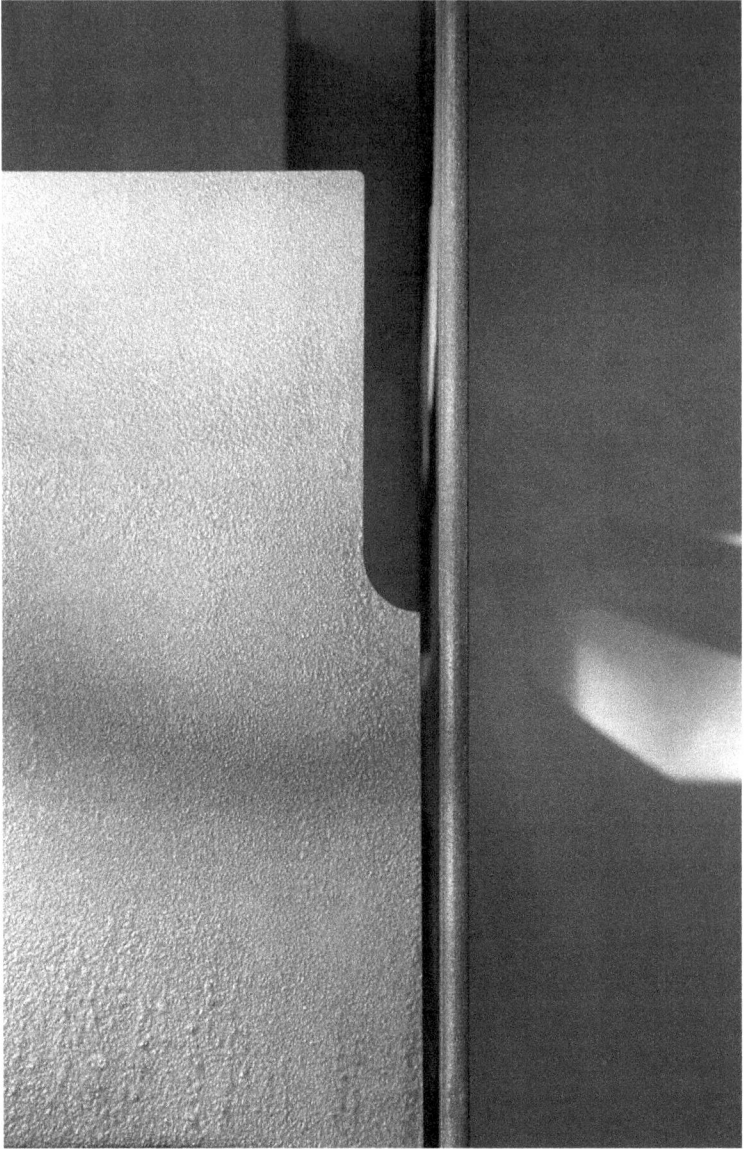

. . . a detail amplifies the depth and broadens the range of sensual experience of hand and eye . . .

4. Details

The meaningful detail is the exception—the detail that forms articulation within the abstraction, demonstrates an inner force within the abstract form, describes joinery within the totality, expresses weight in an immaterial abstraction, or tells us the size of the scaleless building.

—Edward Ford[4]

There was a moment in the process of walking, imagining, and designing, when the towering void in the woods, as seen from the granite dome, first suggested upward flight and the wings of a butterfly—and in an unconscious leap suggested an upswept *pavilion* (by way of etymology: *papillon* in French), but leaving aside thought of the overall design that eventually emerged, I would like now to consider a detail that offers a microcosm of the design process.

---

[4] Edward Ford, *Five Houses, Ten Details*, (New York: Princeton Architectural Press, 2009), p. 238.

The steel shear wall serves the important structural purpose of resisting shearing forces initiated by wind transmitted from the fragile butterfly wing of a roof into the building frame and walls. The steel wall keeps the building square. As a detail it functions as an "autonomous detail." This is to say that as a building element the wall stands apart from and among many other more common elements, and through difference and contrast is a source of architectural meaning, without communicating explicitly. Through its singularity, according to Ford's conception, the "autonomous detail" amplifies the depth and broadens the range of the sensual experience of hand and eye. As part of the design process, this was not a premeditated formal detail, but rather a discovery—a hard found solution to a structural problem.

. . . not a premeditated formal detail, but a discovery . . .

After most of the design decisions had been made, and the drawings were mostly done, the design was continuously tested. How would the spaces feel? What about windows, walls, materials, enclosures, ceilings, colors, and light? What about proportions, heights and dimensions, physical relationships, separations and connections between spaces? From the completed drawings I measured out the rooms and ceiling heights both at home in Cincinnati and in the undistinguished rental house where we stayed on Deer Isle that year. I compared them to long experience, and to what in imagination we hoped by next year would be our house.

Todd had spent the first part of the summer cutting in our road and installing utilities. It was now possible to simply drive in on our own new road. This was an exciting development, for one thing because it became clear, once the woods were cleaned up, how a natural entrance framed the road between an old apple tree and an old stone foundation. It was easy now to come and go. Todd and I staked out the basic outline of the house, sixteen feet by seventy-two feet, extending from north to south. Before we went home that summer Todd's crew excavated down to ledge in order to determine exactly what the foundation contractor would need to build around and over.

And the structural engineer, Dan McGraw, entered the picture. One day Todd and I drove up to Dan's on back roads, winding for an hour through fog and old villages. We parked on a neat and expansive crushed stone driveway, where Dan welcomed us warmly. I later realized that Dan had at first appeared taller than he was. He had greeted us from a wood deck that was six inches higher than the driveway where we stood. In reality he was physically compact in a way that expressed supreme competence about questions of durable structure.

Dan's was an old farmhouse with a barn built close to it, which formed a small entry courtyard. Everything about the house was maintained to be crisp and new, painted white, while the barn was a neat but weathered cedar-shingled antique.

From the deck we climbed the stairs to Dan's well-ordered office, where we talked a bit in that apparently aimless but greeting "how's-the-weather?" sort of way that usually precedes a first business meeting, and then we turned to the project. Dan walked me through the plan, explaining the various conditions that required some special attention. Todd listened. Many sections of exterior wall had been reduced to little more than pilasters two feet wide, and I had repeated this minimal amount of structure in bay after bay along the long west wall of the house so that I could use lots of large sliding glass doors that would look out through the woods to the water. The largest sections of glass were ten feet high by ten feet wide and between them each of the narrow pilasters required steel bracing. In the other short direction, the width of the house, Dan identified a number of sections of wall in which he needed to conceal more shear bracing, also of relatively simple design.

Though I hadn't fully anticipated the need for these concealed steel elements the fix was relatively simple; this was a normal outcome from a first meeting between an architect and an engineer, whose respective skills were necessary to design any but the simplest structure.

But then Dan began to move his pen over the line between the kitchen and the living room and talk about the need for resistance to shear there too. I felt foolish, but also interested, as this was always a special line of transition in the plan. I felt that perhaps I should have more fully anticipated the structural requirement in this area.

. . . a long, hollow tube, with nothing to resist the wind . . .

Dan explained that he had tried different solutions and the simplest and most obvious would be to make a moment frame that would resist the shear. A steel beam could be completely hidden in the ceiling, but columns would protrude from the walls by about eight inches.

The bumps in the walls would wreck everything—there has to be another way. Dan was not surprised; he anticipated I might not like the solution.

Six thousand pounds of shear force would need to be resisted in that area according to a computer generated diagram of the moment frame. Dan had identified a significant structural problem in the design—he just couldn't figure out how to address it without a disruption to the design intention.

I tried to explain my thinking in the broadest possible terms in hopes that we could approach the issue with a fresh perspective and search for a solution together. We sat and stared at the piece of paper.

The imperatives were to resist the wind that would be trying to tear the building apart, to keep open the space held by the building, and to keep the box square. The problem was that I had arranged the building as a long, hollow tube, with nothing to resist the wind that would press fiercely on the walls and roof in a storm—I knew from my own research into weather data, and my own experience, that the winds could come from any direction, from many directions even in a single day. The solution would have to be a choice of a moment frame, x-bracing, a solid or mostly solid wall, or a well-placed shear plate joining the girders at each floor level together and binding these integrally to the foundation.

A steel shear plate could be half an inch or so thick. It could be castellated, with holes in it, provided the holes were well distributed. Ideally the openings would be rounded, but a lot of the plate could be taken away, making it open. Dan began to sketch on a piece of paper and I could see immediately that he was less comfortable sketching, that he would rather generate facts on the computer, but I knew what he meant, that it could have rounded openings, and I began to imagine possibilities.

Peggy and I had once talked back and forth about the area at the end of the kitchen where the floor dropped down two feet. Peggy had argued for something solid and enclosing, like a slatted wood wall. I had objected, and I didn't really understand why this interested her, but I thought that perhaps it might be revived in working out the details of a steel shear wall.

Dan suggested the steel could be cut with a computer driven water jet and that it would not be expensive. I imagined complex filigrees, drawings made from photographs of natural objects: leaves, twigs, stones—a sort of allover lace cut in steel. I could picture the specific qualities of the material. Steel plate was a perfect choice, for already I had been thinking of using a sheet of steel as a hearth, to slide up the wall behind the woodstove, and another sheet of steel in front of the kitchen sink, range, and cabinets. These sheets, proximal to one another, would be dark and rough—they'd speak to each other. In contrast to the light wood interior they would be finished in rust and mill scale, and the history of their handling would be preserved in a raw and natural state. They might look a bit as if they had been found rather than made. Then I flashed on something far simpler than a complex filigree: a large oval opening.

I said much of this out loud to Dan and Todd. Maybe it would sound weird to an engineer or builder. After all, what did mill scale and rust and ovoid shapes have to do with resisting six thousand pounds of shear force? But I could see it: a half-inch thick plate of steel, uniformly rusted and sealed, a dark sienna brown, with the six-foot tall, flawlessly cut shape of an egg. If only the achievement of silence in architecture were always so sudden and unexpected. It is usually more like a long, slow slog up a hill with a backward-looking, sweat-cursed ending. A lot more work had to be done before my ovoid vision became a functioning shear wall and the autonomous detail anchoring the house.

⌛

Edward Ford concludes *The Architectural Detail,* and thus the life's work that preceded it, with meaningful anticlimax when he writes, "Detailing is the act of varying the distance." With this apparently simple statement he unites the process of detailing with the experience of distance and proximity. Designing, the architect zooms or changes scales to get a grip on the big picture and the details; walking, the person experiencing a building sees first from afar then close enough to touch. Detail, Ford tells us, gives architecture meaning.

There are bad details and good details: Ford sorts the difference with five "definitions," that are not so much definitions as explorations of questions yielding a phenomenology of details and detailing. First, he questions the idea of many contemporary practitioners that "there are no details," in the sense that details are not particularly controllable, should be made consistent, or minimized. Second, Ford pursues the idea of details as "motifs," which are subject to failure as mere decorations or fragments. Third, he questions the commonplace notion that details are representations of structure and/or construction. Fourth, Ford explores the idea of details as joints. Especially good details become animated or dissonant, which leads to the fifth and final idea, that of the autonomous or subversive detail that does not resolve but articulates contradiction, acknowledging that we perceive and "respond to architecture in multiple and contradictory ways." In Ford's critique, a great many ordinary details are necessary to make buildings function, but details are only meaningful when they rise to the level of being animated or subversive.

⧗

Hours, days, and weeks later, after my enthusiasm for the egg shape had cooled, I wondered why it had seemed so profoundly perfect at the time. I have learned from experience it is possible to hold absurd, embarrassing ideas in high and serious esteem for far too long. Perhaps it was merely a temporary conquest of intellect by intuition. It felt like a flash of insight, it felt like the right idea, at least for a little while, but then it came to seem a bit stupid, really—a bad idea—because it was so one-dimensional. It felt like a commercial graphic, a bit kitschy, and it would not wear well over time. In hindsight, even in the initial moments of imagining the rusty egg I had wondered if it might be ridiculous. Perhaps this was muddled thinking and muddled intuition.

I was not prepared for what Peggy would say when I described the shear wall idea to her. I explained how it could be cut from a thick steel plate, how it could be left in a raw state, how the water jet could cut anything. I explained to her what castellated means: that we could cut a very large hole in the shear wall and it would still work, especially if the hole was rounded.

Maybe that piece of information was leading, because Peggy surprised me by saying we could cut out the shape of a giant egg. Why had she arrived at the same idea? Did this prove it was a good idea or, on the contrary, that it was no more than the first, most obvious thing? We had both struck on it so quickly. Perhaps it was merely the worst idea, and not the best. Maybe it was only a point of beginning. Or perhaps there was something archetypal about it that would lead more than one person to the same thought.

Deep down, Peggy must have known the egg was not such a good idea. Early on, she had argued for some kind of a screen between the kitchen and the main living area, along the natural line of the floor level change. I liked the strangeness and danger of a lack of a railing. But the need for a shear wall reinvigorated her interest in the screen. In the wake of the engineer's news, she kept making sketches on small slips of paper that showed the panel cut into a series of horizontal slats.

In the mornings in the rental house I usually sat at the kitchen table downstairs in front of the large picture window flanked by two double-hung windows. Rain flowed on the glass one morning, casting a veil of rivulets over everything just outside and across the cove: the sky, the band of spruce and hardwood trees, the sheds and houses, the plane of still water in the cove studded with dozens of lobster boats, a handful of sailboats. It was an insistent rain. Behind me the water sloshed and rattled through the downspout outside the kitchen window.

One of Peggy's small slips of paper lay before me, a se-ries of nine horizontal openings, with some suggested di-mensions. She now slept upstairs, her head pressed into the pillow. She had handed me the slip of paper, declaring it finished, and I had looked at it and remarked that I thought it would work. Secretly I felt differently, that it stinks and she thinks it's good because it's straightforward and therefore pure. I might settle for the idea on the grounds of simplicity and clarity, but I hoped for a more beautiful and interesting solution. Still, we needed a solution and a conclusion—this particular design issue had so far had a protracted and seemingly exaggerated life.

⌛

Our time in Maine over, we were back home in Cincinnati. Several weeks had passed since the shear wall had first arisen as a concern. We went back to work and school. Dan McGraw produced and mailed to me diagrammatic foundation and framing plans that definitively answered most of the structural questions. Dan had math on his side. In contrast, my own drawings served to allow me to obsess over particular conditions, to revisit decisions already made, and to peer deeply into questions of material relationships and subtle adjustments to composition. I felt pressure to finish revising my own drawings, too, so that the architectural and engineering drawings agreed, and so that Todd could proceed to complete his cost estimates and to build the foundation with confidence. We already had a hole in the ground, but still did not know what the shear wall would look like. Resolution could be delayed for a while longer, but it is best to try to push forward on all parts of a design because it is all too easy to remain sweetly delusional. It has to work in physical space and material as well as in airy dream.

Having no solution for the shear wall, having considered and drawn versions of the egg, Peggy's horizontal slats, and round-cornered rectangles, I decided at last to try a different approach.

It was a Saturday, early in September: a good day to begin. Surrounded by 25 yards of white sign painter's bond, 42 inches wide, a tub of black acrylic paint, a roll of black paper, and a glue stick, I set out to make a full-scale drawing. I thought I could then photograph it and convert it on the computer into a cutting pattern for the steel.

Images in books: sculptures by David Smith, Japanese cut paper stencils, and mid-century Scandinavian textile design. I was particularly interested in a 1957 textile by Arne Jacobsen, composed of squares and rectangles placed rather freely in the field, with the warp of the textile serving as an integral control—a pattern that was both geometrically rich and also straightforward and simple. I was intrigued by, but dismissed as too difficult a precedent, a nineteenth century Japanese cut paper stencil that looked a bit like marbled paper. All of these suggested the possibility of a screen that would feel hand-wrought, even if cut by water jet.

The next day, Sunday, we turned the design of the shear wall into a family project. On big sheets of paper in the driveway Peggy painted big circles and swoops that reminded me of Calder. Callie dipped her feet in purple paint and walked across the page. From the kitchen, where I spent the better part of an hour taping two pieces of paper together and drawing out a grid of lines to represent the eight foot tall by six foot, four inch wide shear wall, I watched this activity from a distance. On the lawn Hugh played with the hose, taking off his clothing in stages.

Down in the basement I bent over a huge sheet of paper and painted with David Smith's lines in mind, lines like handwriting that bumped up and down and seemed to speak to each other. Each curve of the brush informed the next curve. Eighteen inches and a few minutes into the attempt it seemed like a promisingly intuitive unfolding of solids and voids.

Arne Jacobsen, textile design, 1957

Japanese cut paper stencil, nineteenth century,
Victoria and Albert Museum, London

But two and a half lines, barely a quarter of the page later it was a perplexing mess of lines and loops. Who did I think I was? Did I really think that I could simply approach a big piece of paper with a brush full of black paint and create something beautiful? Well, yes. Why not? Perhaps, I thought, the human being—the human animal—craves beauty, knows beauty intuitively. Maybe desire for beauty is encoded in our DNA, the length and the arc of the arm, the very way we process visual signals. Perhaps beauty serves mysterious purposes, delivered in abundant surprise.

Or not. I dropped my brush on the page. I was disgusted for indulging the delusion that I could make something beautiful in paint without the painter's skill and long practice with the brush.

⧗

Later that day I began to feel more firmly something that I have thought for a long time: that architects, more than most artists, are collagists and assemblers. We do not so much create, in some kind of pure sense of the word, as put together; we do not so much make as look, examine, and critique.

When looked at this way, architecture, if it is an art, is an art of assemblage, which means that it is also easier to see architecture as a craft—a craft potentially full of artistry and ideas—but a craft nonetheless. It is no longer necessary to dichotomize art and craft, nor to come down firmly on one side or another of unhelpful split thinking. Architecture can first and foremost be craft, with craft's connotations of usefulness and skill, and if it is beautiful, or artful, so much the better.

. . . beauty serves mysterious purposes,
delivered in abundant surprise . . .

To expand this line of thinking it is worthwhile to recognize that some of the best architecture is found, not made. Walk into a clearing in the forest and behold a cathedral—an actual cathedral, not a mere metaphor or symbol of one. The world is filled with architectures of such "artlessness," or "emptiness of intention," to recall Michael Benedikt's phrasing. Bernard Rudofsky called it *Architecture Without Architects*, in his "introduction to non-pedigreed architecture" of the same title. Children know such architectures with their forts and found bush huts that adults lose sight of as they age. Primitive and romantic and nostalgic are some of the words used to cut such found architectures down to size, and cut we humans must for often our prideful works pale in comparison to the humblest natural ones.

⌛

Using blueprint paper, the old-fashioned reactive paper architects used to use to duplicate pencil or ink drawings before the advent of the computer, we began to make sun prints. We arranged flowers, sticks, blades of grass, sea glass, stones, and shells. I made a template so that everything that went on the page fit within the six-foot-four by eight-foot tall area of the shear wall at a scale of 1" =1'-0". Peggy became particularly obsessed with horizontal arrangements. She snipped finger-length shards of ornamental grasses from our yard and placed these carefully, with no pieces touching, and pressed them under glass before taking them into the sun (and the wind). She arranged row upon row of razor clam shells—six, then seven to a page. These, because they were curved, broken-edged, and translucent, developed an oceanic aura on the page.

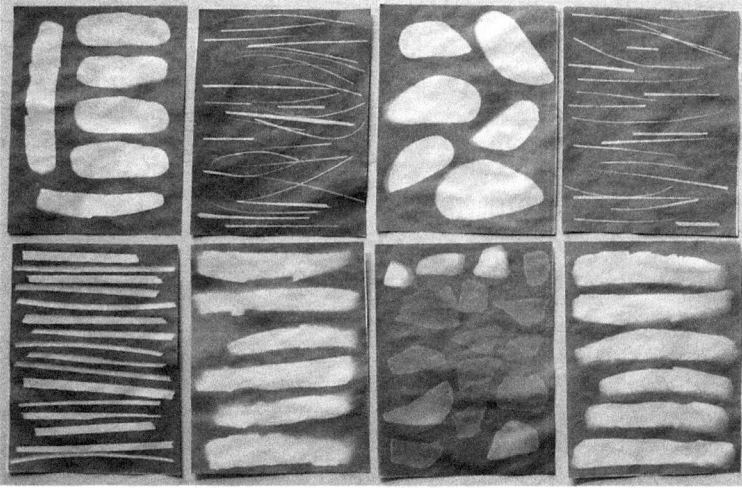

. . . blades of grass, sea glass, stones, and shells . . .

As the making of the sun print shear wall designs proceeded late into Sunday afternoon, I resorted to a simple pencil sketch, also at 1”=1’-0”, of a shape that had been on my mind for a long time, an asymmetrical ovoid that took up most of the sheet, reminiscent of a shape by the 20th century French-German artist Jean Arp. This re-kindled my obsession with the idea of an opening embodied in the egg. Perhaps, I thought, if the ovoid opening was not shaped exactly like an egg it might work.

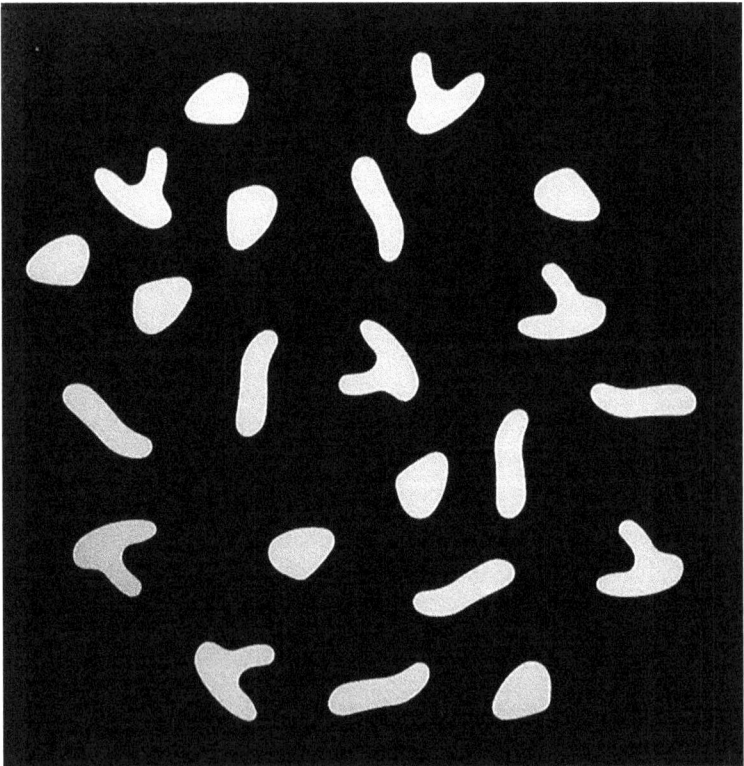

Jean Arp, multiple, 1964

. . . an ovoid opening not shaped exactly like an egg . . . .

There are times in the process of design when one feels compelled to return to the most straightforward idea one can imagine, so I drew an x-brace. I laid it next to the Arp-ovoid on the long window bench in the dining room. Next to these Peggy laid out the drying sun prints. It was a Sunday evening and the light was fading outside. It was time to relax a bit and consider what we had produced. It was time to see if anything in the mess of paintings, drawings, and sun-prints might hold the key to the design of the shear wall.

We liked the razor clams. The outlines of these made horizontal openings in the shear wall. Peggy liked the jagged qualities that showed up in some of the samples, and she also liked the cut blades of grass, but I gravitated to smoothness, to quiet.

As we watched the evening light begin to fade Peggy put our divergent interests in the shear wall in the simplest possible terms, asking if the shear wall is mostly a wall, or if it is mostly an opening. Architects are often thought of and derided for speaking like this—in riddles—but it helps to ask essential and radical questions. We argued this wall/opening question in functional terms: Would the children run through the kitchen and leap off the edge of the floor into the living room?

Callie, spinning around the kitchen floor, waiting for dinner and listening to the strange universe of adult conversation, provided us with the flash of an impish smile, as if to say, "Yes. We will run and jump through the opening."

She often knew which of us was on which side of a discussion and she genuinely seemed to enjoy seeing how our discussion of differences worked out.

We wondered: Would this bother the cook?

At first I said maybe, then I said maybe not, I didn't think so, I wasn't sure. I was trying to be honest and objective, and since I do all of the cooking it was reasonable for me to be uncertain. So this question alone didn't really settle things.

Peggy tried, as a rhetorical strategy, to get me to agree that I would change it the minute some kid played hide-and-seek by leaping through the hole. Of course it couldn't be changed easily after the fact, and I couldn't really argue that a kid wouldn't leap through the hole, so I wouldn't agree. I wouldn't accept the challenge. I knew anyway that this was only an argumentation technique Peggy used in order to win. If you are married to someone long enough you start to see the syntax before it is fully formed and from the syntax you know the intent.

From the beginning Peggy showed not a trace of interest in the large ovoid shape although she criticized it when I hung it up by humming the theme song to *2001: a Space Odyssey*. She just didn't see it the way I saw it. It reminded me of other things: a moon gate in a Zen garden, Jean Arp, an egg. Beautiful things. I was a bit in love with it, perhaps blind in love. But I had to listen, to try to see it as she saw it. What Peggy saw was an opening, but fundamentally she wanted a wall. I had to discern why I might bend to her desire, for I was ever so slightly beginning to do so.

Peggy had argued the relatively straightforward horizontal slat wall but it just wasn't weird enough. Nor did it feel inevitable. But the razor clam—the Atlantic jackknife clam—met my criteria for weirdness. We had collected the shells on the beach in North Carolina ourselves, and they had been in our possession for half of our lives together. I worried—see how nonsensical the thinking of an architect can be? —that the razor clam had nothing to do with Maine. It turns out the Atlantic Jackknife Clam—*Ensis directus*—

is found from Labrador to South Carolina. It looks like a straight razor and grows to a length of seven or eight inches. It can cut instantaneously into sand—a foot or more—at the first sign of disturbance. Perhaps, I thought, it is the shape that helps limit the market attractiveness of the razor clam; do people unconsciously avoid foods that look like they could be used to slit a throat? But no, once vast fisheries of razor clams in New England and Quebec were harvested and canned until they were nearly obliterated.

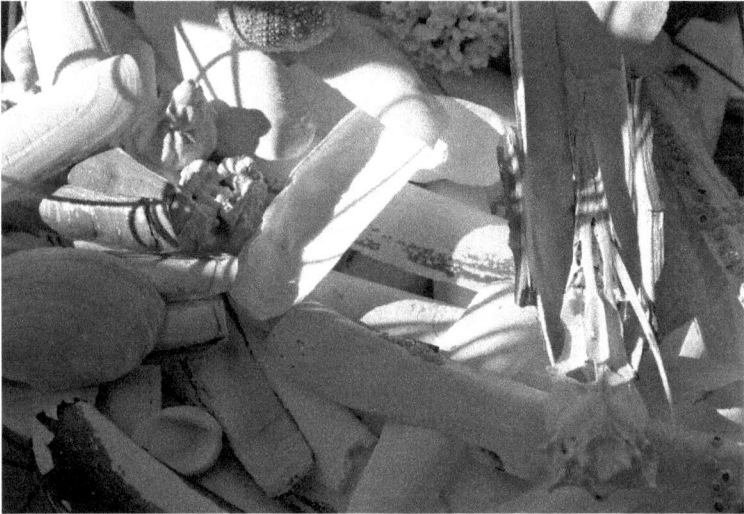

. . . once vast fisheries of razor clams in New England and Quebec were harvested and canned until they were nearly obliterated . . .

The next morning over coffee, reviewing the pile of remaining images, the razor clams were winning; esteem for the ovoid opening had slipped. This playing with shapes and openings in steel had me questioning what we were doing: we were messing with the graphics of a structural element. Something about it felt misguided or impure. A couple of decades ago I attended a presentation by an associate of the architect-theorist-philosopher Christopher Alexander during which he described a process of designing a truss that was not so unlike our messing around with the shear wall. At the end of the presentation a man stood up in the back of the room and claimed, shaking "This is not the art of engineering. This is window dressing, and a shoddy approach to it at that." His voice rose in anger as he explained that *good* engineering—the *art* of engineering—can't come from such an approach, but rather must come from a full understanding of the forces involved in a given situation, and the material properties available to address those forces. He cited an example of a particular exemplary engineer—someone with whom he had apparently been associated—and he cited a particular building. "That," he said, "is the art of engineering—the best, most efficient use of material, elegantly arrayed. Not this . . . this is pretzel logic."

Were we indulging in window dressing, mere decorating, in thinking first of what the shear wall would look like, just as that stranger at the Alexander lecture had decried? According to this logic, the right approach is to ask the engineer, what is the most efficient way to build, and then do that—not just with the shear wall, but with the entire building—let efficiency establish the moral code. But efficiency, though admirable, should not be made a god. There is a specific kind of beauty that comes from close contact with the natural world, with contradictions and anomalies that scramble perfection a little. Nature is confusing and contradictory in that way.

Peter Zumthor describes the design process in his studio, where everyone works to fully address every engineering consideration and functional requirement without concern for form. In the process of working these things out they pay attention to what Zumthor describes as his "interests"— light, sound, material, temperature, etc.—but he doesn't worry over form, or imagine form first or early. If the result is not surprisingly beautiful they start the process of design again. This it seems to me is a proper relationship between architecture and engineering.

⧗

Later I called Dan to ask him how much of the wall could be cut away. Would the single ovoid opening make sense, and if so, what kinds of margins would be reasonable? Dan said that we could remove up to about a third of it overall, and the ovoid shape removed something more like two-thirds of the shear wall, so that probably wouldn't work. I asked Dan about a series of horizontal shapes, like the razor clams, long and thin, with maybe a foot of margin on the sides. He said with a drawing he could analyze the actual forces. I would need to get an actual drawing finished.

One night after dinner we sat and reviewed the process of designing the shear wall in hopes of bringing the process to a close. The pleasure of new ideas, like newly discovered species of tropical snails or butterflies or birds, seduce with the promise of more such pleasures.

Thankfully, it seemed the thing had simply and effort-lessly found its form. It sounds a little absurd—the idea that the shear wall, an inanimate slab of steel—would somehow be involved in finding its own form. But really, how else did it come into existence?

Maybe it was only a rationalization: six openings made more sense than seven; the long, narrow proportion of the shells related to the long, narrow proportion of the plan; and in the end, the shear wall was neither opening nor screen but rather poised between the two opposite ideas.

The sun-prints were only the beginning of clarity. Over the next few weeks there were some other steps: hand draw-ing the razor clams, scanning the drawing and translating it into a computer file, attempting to do the same thing on a digital tablet, and plotting a full-sized drawing of the shear wall as a confirmation.

For this I turned to my colleague John Humphries, a brilliant maker of mischief, a bon vivant who believes faithfully in poking fun at life's absurdities and exploiting any situation with good humor. John likes to tell tall tales and half-truths with a twinkle in his eye, and although it sometimes seems to me a bit like the schoolyard be-havior of issuing wet-willies or pulling hair, perhaps I am just too serious. I asked John if he would help me to per-form a digital translation of my hand drawing, which he did generously and happily. An elementary process, John presented me with a graphic showing five different ver-sions arranged from "original to smooth to less smooth to polygonal to more polygonal." We agreed that smooth was the best option, with the most elegant line work, and plotted a full-size drawing of the wall—11'-9" high by 6'-10" wide, including the anchor bolts and flanges that would secure it to structure and allow the shear wall to do its work.

I laid the drawing out on the floor and I could see nuance in the line that was not visible earlier—most notably a quivering in the line at the bottom of one of the cutouts. I asked John about this, and he explained it as "noise," although I suspect that it was much more intentional, a bit of digital mischief. But no matter, it was not unlike the tremor in my hand, a quaver in the original drawings that the digital process had expunged and then restored in a different guise. So it remained; the steel would be cut that way. I like this mischief. It amuses me, and it has a certain kind of intelligence, given that the code that drives the water jet could drive the water jet anywhere, in any way. Though far from random, it is not unlike the apparent anomalies and mutations of code found in nature.

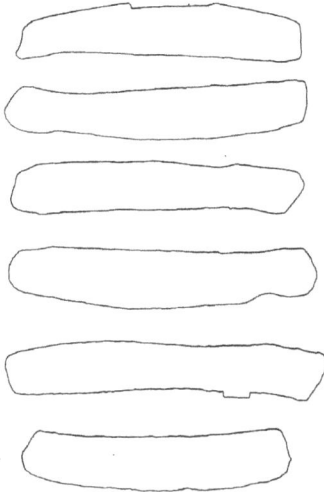

... not unlike the shaking in my hand ...

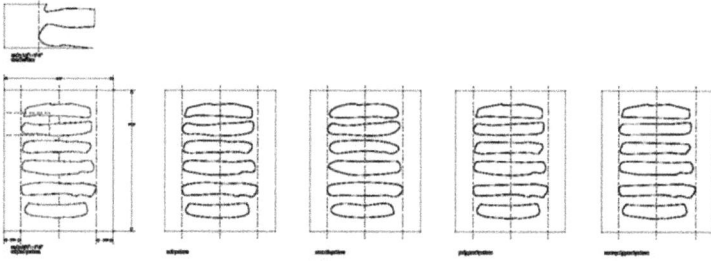

...five different versions...

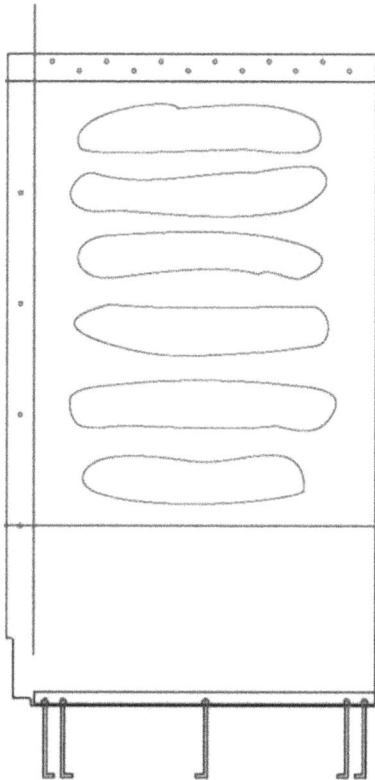

*... to be completely certain of the scale I taped the
full-size drawing up in the living room ...*

To be completely certain of the scale I taped the full-size drawing up in the living room. After all, a person would be standing next to it in the kitchen at one level and two feet lower next to the woodstove. Scale is judged by a feeling in the body, particularly between the elbows and shoulders, if one is sitting down, and between the heels and the top of the head, if one is standing. The rightness of the human scale confirmed, the full-size drawing and computer file were sent to Todd in Maine where the slab of steel would be fabricated and finished.

⧗

Todd sent a series of photographs of the installation of the wall in December. In one it is hanging from the bucket of a backhoe with a guy in heavy canvas work clothes guiding it into position. The steel is lightly dusted with snow. The guy looks attentive to the mechanics of moving steel. In another photograph the workers look concerned about lining things up, matching the holes in the steel to the holes in the wood, and in another they are tightening bolts. They do not look the least bit puzzled by the strangeness of the slab of steel, rather they look intent upon their work.

The limitations and possibilities of the site had led to the arrangement of a long, narrow building. Several steel shear frames had to be employed hidden within walls, but the need to provide for shear resistance at the mid-point of the main space remained, which generated the shear wall and its curious shapes, which became an autonomous detail. Autonomous details commonly create such contrasts, and often in particular ways; as Ford points out, the most common type of autonomous detail involves a "tactile, sculptural, animated intrusion into [a] rigid, abstract, and geometric building." It has a long architectural history, and it occurs in a variety of conditions—it is a detail at odds with the building that contains it.

. . . attentive to the mechanics of moving steel . . .

It is not surprising then, in a building with the simplicity, plainness, and abstraction that comes from regional precedents, that the design of the shear wall would take on forms found in nature. But it also has to do with sculpture proper, a thought that also supported a decision that we had already made: that in spite of our art collecting habits, the building would contain no art, at least in the sense of the conventional categories of pictures and sculpture. Freedom from pictures and sculpture would better render art of the surrounding landscape and waterscape. Specific elements of the interior might begin to blur the lines between nature, building, craft, furnishing, and art proper. A goal for the house would be a more diverse and inclusive world of objects contained within a plain interior, a well-proportioned interior, composed of little more than material of a hue and texture consonant with the forest. Of this decision, friends remarked, "Yes, the landscape will be your art."

Designing the steel shear wall was an intuitive, experimental process, followed by more focused explorations of natural materials through collage. Looking for a balance of opening and surface, a pleasing interplay of line, thinking about particular sculptural and graphic predecessors such as Jean Arp, David Smith, Japanese stencils, and Scandinavian textiles eventually led to the razor clam.

While Ford provides an explanation for the logic of this kind of detail (it is autonomous, animated, and it subverts the abstract and rigid geometry of the rest of the building), Pallasmaa does not (perhaps to better vouchsafe its nobly mysterious origin). Still, some post hoc explanations, in addition to the all-encompassing one provided by Ford, remind me of the phenomenological analysis of Norberg-Schulz that Simon Unwin explains so plainly and explains how to use so pragmatically.

. . . in actual experience, though perhaps not in photographs, the steel shear wall recedes into the background as a quiet plastic presence . . .

Ellsworth Kelly, Stele II, 1973, ©Estate of Ellsworth Kelly, National Gallery of Art, Washington, DC

Over time, reflecting on my own completed work, I have realized several things about the architecture of this detail at the heart of the house. These are realizations supported and clarified by Unwin's "frames of reference for doing." Why does the detail work? First, being made of oxidized steel, it provides color and texture contrast with the surrounding material, which supports the more significant contrast of the differing sense of temperature with wood. Proximity to the woodstove reinforces awareness of the importance of temperature sense. Second, the wall in its form has a particularly humanizing relationship to scale, namely, a foot on the wall equals an inch on the actual razor shell, a proportional relationship that is repeated in the timber bench nearby, which was dimensioned in customary feet-inch scale, relative to an ordinary and familiar six-inch architectural scale. Third, the openings, six in number, reiterate the six-module organization of the house. Fourth, the resulting form is that of both a screen and framing device. It is open and closed, as the forest is open and closed, so it reinforces the larger idea of the room discussed already, namely that it is open especially to breezes, light, and weather. In this way the shear wall is a metaphor of the forest, which undercuts the more literal and sorrowful memory of the nearly vanished razor clams.

In *Eyes of the Skin,* Pallasmaa's initiatory complaint, which is the complaint motivating many another phenomenological perspective, concerns the idea that we no longer experience the world through our bodies and, as Gaston Bachelard famously celebrated in *The Poetics of Space,* the world's *roundness.* For Pallasmaa, a flattening gaze reduces the world and architecture, thus:

As a consequence of the current deluge of images, architecture of our time often appears as mere retinal art, thus completing an epistemological cycle that began in Greek thought and architecture. But the change goes beyond mere visual dominance; instead of being a situational bodily encounter, architecture has become an art of the printed image fixed by the hurried eye of the camera. In our culture of pictures, the gaze itself flattens into a picture and loses its plasticity. Instead of experiencing our being in the world, we behold it from outside as spectators of images projected onto the surface of the retina. David Michael Levin uses the term "frontal ontology" to describe the prevailing frontal, fixated, and focused vision.[5]

The shear wall as a detail would subvert the frontal ontology of which Pallasmaa complains. The room, in its orthogonal, classically proportioned, conventional formality, would seem to have been created by an enthusiast of the picturesque view and yet the steel wall would also be experienced as sculpture. In actual experience, though perhaps not in the photographs, the steel shear wall recedes into the background as a quiet plastic presence, heightening the room's rigidity, enhancing the softness of the ground, the forest, and the waterscape beyond.

Walking in Washington, DC one spring with Callie, Ellsworth Kelly's *Stele II* reminded me of this theme of environmental sculpture and explained in part the steel shear wall to me. The steel shear wall plays with a similar relationship between flatness and plasticity, picture plane and multidimensionality. This is one way that the shear wall works.

---

[5] Juhani Pallasmaa, *The Eyes of the Skin: Architecture and the Senses*, (Chicester, UK: Wiley-Academy, 2005) p. 33.

. . . choose people with the right level of
skill for any particular task . . .

5. Craft

Design is what, for practical purposes, can be conveyed in words and by drawing: workmanship is what, for practical purposes, can not.

—David Pye[6]

Anyone who has ever built a house knows that the selection of the general contractor is critical to the outcome of the work. I chose my contractor, Todd Lawson, based on a recommendation and several meetings to discuss intentions. This was long before I had a design, a town approved site plan, a cleared road—long before I had camped and walked the land. How does one decide about a person? How does one know if the person standing before you is telling the truth or blowing smoke? How does one person's self-repre-

---

[6] David Pye, *The Nature and Art of Workmanship*, (Cambridge, UK: 1968), p.1.

sentation of competence, care, or insight compare with reality? These questions, to me, are a mystery; when it comes to people, one can never be absolutely sure.

But then, it seems Todd chose my project as carefully as I chose him. He seemed sincere, honest, and truthful; I believed that he could deliver what he promised. And years ago, as a young man, Todd had contemplated a career in architecture. He had an apprenticeship of sorts to a Maine architect who was the architect of record for the Haystack Mountain School of Crafts at the time when they were doing their gateway project and auditorium, so Todd was tasked with drawing flashing details. From a certain perspective, water management is ninety-percent of successful architecture and building. Todd understood water management. Above all Todd cared about detail, and this was the most important indicator. As I would eventually learn, one of the things Todd did very well was choose people with the right level of skill for any particular task according to the level of quality required. His judgment about this was based on considerable lifetime experience. Not all contractors care so much about quality or qualities. Todd did.

⌛

After Todd sent me the photographs of the shear wall being installed, I had the opportunity to go to Deer Isle to see the house under construction for the first time. I was in Portland in January, attending a writing residency for ten days, and after that I had time to drive up the coast. The morning I started out snow fell for five hours. Shelves of snow weighed on the black-green spruce boughs, forming walls and rooms along the edge of the highway. Above the trees the dull white sky loomed. Beyond the trees blocks of ice drifted in the lichen-green water of Casco Bay. The road was slick with ice and snowmelt in places, and it was deeply tracked with snow, but ahead an enormous yellow dump truck, lights flashing, plowed the highway, throwing a grey arc to the side of the road. Behind it, the rental car I was driving, a bright blue SUV, whirred along at sixty miles an hour. It was warm inside. The sun in the side view mirror hung white and low in the sky. It's a three-hour drive. Sunset would be in an hour, around 4:30. I would not make it to the house before nightfall.

After dark I would strain to read words on signs, to perceive distance, to sharpen focus on lights and things. Shadows and shapes would bounce around in the dark. I would need to remain awake and keep the car on the road.

In the dark the house would be more like a dream, not a construction project with its myriad details and worries. It was frightening to imagine the house in the dark: an unlit, unfinished, empty house in the woods—blank-eyed and hollow as if abandoned and decayed.

Still, I also imagined the house as it would be finished—lit up in the dark with the snow all around it in the forest at the edge of the cove, the cozy psychological opposite of ruin. And, anxiously, I thought of the large expanse of glass around the living room. Will we feel exposed? Peggy and I had talked through a way of curtaining with one continuous piece of fabric on one continuous track. We had looked at long, elegant curtains while sipping red wine in the lobby of The James hotel in Chicago. We felt warm; beautiful people lounged in that lobby, talking and laughing while snow fell outside among the lights and the taxis. I loved the idea that in our house in the woods what would be an open pavilion in the day would transform into an enveloping tent at night. These two words are intimately related—*pavilion, papillon, butterfly, tent.* It seemed somehow right to keep the memory of the tent, my first habitation on the land, in the finished house.

⧗

Behind me in the side view mirror the sun blazed orange and laid orange-gold on the road and snow. On the turnpike there was a car that had spun out from the opposite lane, but it had slid harmlessly into the three or four feet of snow in the median. On that side of the highway drivers were blinded driving into the sun. Traffic on both sides had come to a crawl, and help was gathering. There was another car spun out fully sideways, a large American sedan, its tail in the deepest part of the median ditch, snow up to the windows. A man I saw in profile in the back seat looked passive; there were four or five adults in the car. They were stuck, they couldn't open the doors, and they would have to wait. There were three or four cars like this all spun out and off the road, with police and tow trucks gathering.

⧗

I drove into the last of the twilight, off the turnpike, onto the back roads, and sped through tunnels of trees, then open fields, facing headlights. There were nineteenth century farmhouses set right on the road, ranch houses and trailers set farther back. There were plowed driveways and deep piles of snow. Part of the sky was still bright behind me and to the right, though it wouldn't last long. It would not stay bright long enough for me to get there. In that part of the drive the landscape begins to open out into long rolling waves of land. The Atlantic Ocean lay beyond to the right and up ahead. Up ahead, too, was Cadillac Mountain—or at least that's what I thought it was—and it looked for a moment like the only possible destination, but then it was gone somewhere behind trees and the shifting shapes of land.

The moon! Huge and orange, slightly compressed from top to bottom, perhaps one day past full. It sped and hid and reappeared. The moon lit up the landscape—perhaps I could go to the house in the dark after all, there would be moonlight . . . though there would also be long and frightening shadows cast on the snow through the trees.

⌛

Up ahead there were lights beyond my headlights, the dark hulk of a house off to the right, a light slowly flashing as if disappearing and reappearing behind trees, but too fast, and too regular, like a warning. I slowed the car. There were three figures standing. The slowly flashing light was a flashlight being swung back and forth by a hooded woman looking straight toward me. There was an enormous deer in the road, flayed open, red at the neck, headless. The people standing there were simply warning drivers, waiting for help to get the carcass off the road. I felt admiration for these neighbors standing out in the cold, but it would be foolish for me to stop to offer my help. The meat would not be wasted.

⌛

I didn't know where I was in the dark. There was something that looked like a mill stack studded with lights, and there was an enormous cloud rising, and just as I noticed another line of lights arrayed in a long horizontal line with a slight arc I realized the great cloud was rising into the sky from beyond a cliff. The cloud looked explosive.

I had arrived at the new Penobscot Narrows Bridge, with its observation room in one of the two 420 foot tall towers. The cliff I had seen was where the granite was blasted away to bring the curved approach road through. I would cross two bridges tonight. Penobscot Narrows would be the first, and it is more than two thousand feet long, but the second is far scarier. The Deer Isle-Sedgewick Bridge, built in 1939, suffered wind damage while under construction, so additional cables were added from the main suspension cables to the cross bracing on the towers. A couple of years later it was damaged again, some of the additional cables broke, and a new round of improvements ensued. It is a cobweb of cables, the result of trial and error and repair.

Repair work and maintenance on the bridge was recently ongoing for several years and now it was nearly finished. One Deer Isle shopkeeper once told me teenagers used to drive up and park on the bridge to feel it sway back and forth. More than one islander told me they expected the bridge to collapse at any time, and that is one reason to keep a good boat working. It is in many respects similar to the Tacoma Narrows Bridge, also known as "Galloping Gertie," known by every high school physics student through the classroom film and now the YouTube video that shows it swaying, the roadbed buckling, and one Professor Farquharson risking his life for a dog in a car. The Tacoma Narrows Bridge collapsed four months after completion in 1940 in a forty-two mile per hour wind. The potential for a similar fate has been on the mind of people crossing the Deer Isle-Sedgewick Bridge ever since.

When I arrived at the bottom of the Deer Isle bridge I summoned my courage and went. I drove gripping the wheel, watched the road and the speedometer, and kept the car at twenty-five miles an hour. It is a sharp angled upward drive to the top, then a moment on the crown, then a sharp slope down to land again. It was made high so as not to impede yacht traffic through Eggemoggin Reach. In the daytime it feels like climbing into the sky on a thin wire and then passing through a fragile iron gate of dizzying height into eternal nothingness. At night it is only a passage of blind concentration.

I was off the bridge and in the last miles to the house— only six miles to Stonington where I would spend the night. I only had the causeway to cross, then a short drive up the hill and I'd be on Deer Isle proper. The causeway is an S-shaped section of road lined with jagged boulders. There is a beach to the right, and the channeled, windy waters of Eggemoggin Reach to the left. I once had lunch with Todd and Curt Haskell in the Harbor Cafe, and they were telling stories. Todd says, "A guy parks his truck on Causeway Beach, backs it down to launch a boat, takes off and returns a few hours later and finds his truck submerged to the top of the cab." Curt nods, and in an even more deadpan tone than Todd, finishes the story: "That was how he learned about tides."

At the Irving station, and the left turn toward Sunshine and the house, I had to decide quickly. The moon was bright overhead, the sky perfectly clear. A left turn. It was just another mile. In the summer I turn in to the road on the right and open all the car windows and let the car creep along and I breathe and listen to the engine purr.

At the road I turned right and opened the driver's side window and drove slowly listening to the scrunch of packed snow and the crisp silence of the trees. The cold poured in. Would the neighbors see the headlights and wonder who was here at night? Though dark it was only six-thirty—hardly an evildoer's hour. The road was freshly plowed; there were piles and shards of snow along the edge. Shadows streamed into the woods and moonlight lit up the snow.

At the house the headlights lit up the wall of sheathing and cast deep shadows into the rectangular opening and beyond into the woods and onto the deep snow rising up over the buried dome of granite. I got out of the car and walked toward the front door. The snow was deep and light and it fell in on top of my shoes as I walked. I walked carefully, looked into the door at the concrete foundation wall and the shapes of things beneath the drifts of snow. I looked beyond the house into shadow, and turned around. It was too hazardous to go any further in the dark. I did not know what pieces of steel or planks of wood may lie hidden beneath the snow. I couldn't see anything in the shadows beyond the bright headlights. I would have to wait until morning to see the house.

⌛

Before dawn at the Inn on the Harbor in Stonington, there was a sliver of blue-red fire on the horizon just beyond the long, low islands. The light illuminated the sky and the shingled walls of the proud, compact, gabled houses. A single lobster boat cut across the flat water, sharpening the clarity of cold silence. Just enough snow had been shoveled out along a path to expose the ice encrusted wood deck beneath.

It was slow going to walk across the glassy, rippled ice in the bitter cold.

After some toast and coffee in the office I settled my bill and inched out through the cold to the car. It felt like such a long drive back to the house, down and then up the deep hills. Anticipation swallowed everything. The whole morning was still suffused with light, though the soft blue-red had given way to a brighter yellow-white that now flared through the trees. Parking the rental car in the turnaround, I got out, tested the ground for ice, and walked carefully. Though warmly dressed, with warm socks, long underwear, blue jeans, long-sleeved cotton shirt, fleece pullover, jacket, scarf, gloves, and my warmest hat, it was cold enough that my eyes stung with tears. To see the house clearly I wiped them with the rough back of my glove. There was ice on the road so I walked slowly. I slid, even walking carefully. I didn't want to fall.

I was mindful that I would be entering the actual house for the first time, at least the rough shell of it. Now I could actually see it. The shape of the north elevation was now complete, though the sheathing was unfinished, and the roof, though partly framed, was open. The girders drew the right-ward-upward-westward gesture of the roof and then there was only bare framing for six feet below the highest point. The sunlight cut through the trees and laid yellow-white triangles of light on the long east wall of the house. I felt excited. There it was! The exterior was sheathed in orange panels. Only two openings were cut into the north wall. I wondered what it would look like when all of the openings were cut in.

I walked deliberately on the compacted snow and ice. I wanted to register the significance of this first walk up to the house. Until then the house had existed only in my imagination and the abstraction of drawings. Now it began to exist, and would begin to exist in memory.

My idea had always been to close in the road from the turnaround to the house with small trees and ferns, cultivated from those in the woods, so that it would feel more like a path or trail rather than a road. At the end of the trail there would be a raised wood walkway sloping up to the entry. But on that first visit there were trucks, a dumpster, and a portable toilet in the way. The excavator had laid down gravel to make a temporary road and a flat platform so that trucks and equipment and supplies could come and go, and all of this gravel was covered in ice and snow. A crane had been set up there a week before, driven up from the boatyard in Stonington, and used to lift the roof girders into position. Imagining what the road would feel like when the house was finished was hard, it had been easier before the terrain was altered and all these things were put in the way.

. . . the idea had always been to close in the road
from the turnaround to the house . . . so that it
would feel more like a path or a trail . . .

There was a place to the right after the road dipped down and began to return upwards toward the house where the woods opened a clear view to the water. The trees overturned there in a storm the winter before, blasting almost all the way through to the cove. At the end of the open area there was a remnant of the storm—a single spruce trunk with its top half snapped off—the limbs lay half-buried in the snow, and beyond it was the watery plate of the cove.

Now I had to step into deep snow and lift my feet high with every step. The snow was light and crisp and full of air. I heard workers on the other side of the wall inside the house. I stopped at the opening to the porch and looked through to the front door. I could see through to the openings and the pilasters supporting the west wall of the house, and beyond that were trees and snow. Though it lay buried in snow, the exterior deck was framed, and there were many tall sections of scaffolding erected on it.

It didn't make much sense for me to try to step into the area of the porch as if entering the house, for if I did I would be standing at least two feet below the level of the floor deck. I had to be content to walk around the house. I was curious about how the main floor level related to the dome of granite, the "big rock," though it was difficult to tell, because everything was buried in snow. Still, this wasn't really a time for worry; there were some things I would not have been able to see then. It was better to just look.

One of the workers stepped into view on the main floor deck, stepped down into the snow, and said hello. He volunteered that Brian, the boss, was up on the second floor. When he said hello he said, predictably I thought, "You must be the owner." We shook gloved hands and exchanged names. His name was Walter. I looked at his face and I felt I already knew something about him. Beneath his glasses he was bleary-eyed, and I thought that although he looked like he was in his forties, he was probably much younger. He was carrying a green plastic bottle of Mountain Dew and smoking a cigarette. When he smiled I could see that he was missing a couple of upper teeth. He was wearing a hat similar to mine, though his was made of sheepskin, and he was wearing heavy canvas Carhartt overalls, and enormous rubber work boots that looked like they were well insulated. Although he seemed to think that the very first thing I wanted to do was talk to Brian, nothing could be further from the truth. I could tell right away—in fact I had always known from the few photographs Todd had sent me—that the people building the house were doing an excellent job. I had no need to check up on workers. I really just wanted to walk around and look, and for that I did not need a guide.

I stepped up on a large block of wood onto the plywood floor deck. The shear wall was surrounded by equipment, lengths and blocks of framing lumber, rectangles of plywood, boxes of framing hardware, yellow power cords, a green steel gang-box, a ladder, and some crumpled blue tarps. An aluminum snow shovel and a scaffolding walk-board leaned against the shear wall; a yellow work-light hung from one of the razor clam openings.

The edge that lets down into the living room was mostly bare plywood and the lower floor was white with snow and sunlight. It was a pronounced but exaggerated difference. There were six sawhorses on the deck, each covered in a couple of inches of snow, and they were all standing in drifted snow. The trees beyond the openings were draped in snow. From where I stood my first impression was that the space was too tall, too narrow, and far too open all around. I felt worried that I had made a grave error and I would have to live with it. I worried whether it was right to make the ceiling ten feet high and I stepped down into the space.

From experience I know that buildings under construction go through weird transformations: the viewer's perceptions shift dramatically in response to what is actually there. In general, open floor decks without walls seem the right size—after all, you have spent so much time establishing correct dimensions that it could hardly be otherwise. When framed, buildings go through a horrible constriction—the repetitive and rhythmic grip of the sticks of lumber does this. When finished, the size and scale of things return to normal. Normal, that is, if you got them right in the first place. It helps to remember these phase shifts during construction. Though uneasy at first, I thought that perhaps I would feel more comfortable with the scale and proportion of the room in time.

Standing in the drifted snow on the plywood deck in what would be our living room felt like standing in the forest. Though the forest was quite still, the air moved through unimpeded. Outside the drapery of spruce boughs covered in snow suggested the limits of a larger room, making a room within a room. Directly in front, and to each side of the rectangular room within the forested room, there was an opening ten feet wide and ten feet high, into which would fit pairs of sliding doors flanked by sidelights, beneath a transom. I tried to imagine how the feeling of the space would change when the glass and its substantial wood frame was in place. This would change the scale and sense of enclosure for the better. In summer, in fine weather, the doors would open and the air would move through the screens so that we would feel out-of-doors.

To the south and the west we would step out onto a six-foot wide wood deck. Stairs would descend around several moss-covered boulders to the duff-covered ground, but none of this was visible now, for it was incomplete and buried in snow. Todd's men had poured the concrete piers and built the deck framing some time ago so that it could be used to erect the scaffolding that now rose in a chaos of rusty steel tubes and x-bracing higher than the door openings.

The steel shear wall seemed both ordinary and extraordinary. The water jet had made a fine cut the edge of the opening along the line described by the computer, itself a version of my freehand line. There were fine striations perpendicular to the face of the steel where the water and graphite had drilled through the steel. It was perfect. The leading edge of the sheet of steel was ever so slightly rounded over, a nice touch, a good refinement for which I am grateful because it makes the object better.

A couple of days before seeing the shear wall I had talked on the phone with Curt Haskell, the electrical contractor from Stonington. Curt is a red-faced, jovial looking fellow. He is bespectacled and unserious looking, but this belies the truth, for he is a highly respected and accomplished business owner, first-rate electrician, a solid member of the community, and smart and curious. In that conversation Curt asked me a series of questions about what kinds of fixtures I wanted to use and how I wanted to switch them. I answered as thoroughly as possible but we agreed we would have to resolve some things at the house. There came a point in our discussion when we had wrapped up most of the details, then he asked, "What about that shear wall?" Surprised, I responded, "What about it?" The defensive edge in my voice must have sounded like, "None of your business." He seemed to collect himself, then asked, "Well, is there any electrical in that area?" a question that returned us to the practical matters at hand. "Well, there are the floor outlets, and the one outlet in the center of the plywood at the floor level change, but nothing having to do with the shear wall."

What he was thinking, what he wanted to know, or what sort of conversation he wanted to have about the shear wall I'll never know, for I effectively shut down any kind of conversation. My mistake. I'd really like to know. I wonder, what does a man like Curt think when he steps into the house and sees this thing? On some level it must look perfectly insane to him—this talk about the shapes of razor clams—but beyond that, what is he thinking? What does he see?

⧗

One day soon after I returned home to Cincinnati from Maine, Peggy, Callie, and Hugh were out on an errand, so I had the house to myself. I wandered around and looked at the pictures on the walls and I realized I had not looked at them for a while. Many of the pictures came to me after my parents died, when we three brothers each took a turn choosing what we wanted to take, in a common ritual of grieving and moving on.

Some family members argue over possessions, and nurse hurt feelings for years, but not us. At the time I felt certain that my mother had carefully orchestrated our harmony, both before she died, in the kinds of questions and answers she gave me that never felt like instructions, and after she died, from a mysterious, faraway place.

My parents were not wealthy people. My father had a high-flying job with LIFE magazine until I was twelve years old when LIFE laid off hundreds of staff including my dad. Everything fell apart for us with the economic malaise of 1973 to 1975. My parents had a hard time paying the most basic bills, but they taught me to look at art. It was a contradictory and confused upbringing.

Now I wandered around and looked at the pictures on the walls: a Robert Motherwell print—a vigorous gesture in black ink that my father loved, that my children said looked like "a cow pooping North America"; a scribbly drawing by Katherine Porter; two small early paintings and a huge canvas by my parents' friend John Hultberg—all three blue; a beautiful print by Karl Schrag that my parents gave me before they died: "Red Sun-Dark Woods"—it always reminds me of the Fourth of July; and a Louise Nevelson wood construction from the early 1950s that has pieces of driftwood in it, called "Adrift."

And then there was the Jean Arp multiple: an edition of 100 from the Walker Art Center, Minneapolis, circa 1966. White shapes on a black felt square under Plexiglas about the size of a record album—each of the one hundred owners could arrange the shapes, making one hundred unique and flexible compositions.

When my father received the Arp he traced the shapes on paper so I could play with them. The black square of felt lay on the surface of the golden oak table, beneath the painted green and gold-leafed chandelier. I made a cowboy on a horse, while my father arranged abstractly, which was an approach I imagine I did not much appreciate. It was after dark, and the dining room windows reflected us seated at the table beneath the blazing chandelier. Outside beyond the glass was blue-black twilight and tree shadow. It felt good sitting next to my father arranging shapes.

I still keep the Arp on my wall the way my father arranged it those many years ago. It is a beautiful field of shapes, just as he saw it.

⧗

The end of another semester and then we counted the weeks until the children would be finished with school and it would be time to head off to Deer Isle, this time to stay in our own newly finished house. After a few weeks there, we would be going to Luxembourg to teach for a year and to travel in Europe. There were many details to be taken care of: school enrollments, course planning, final travel arrangements, immigration documents. To me it was frustrating to think we would get the house finished, see it briefly, and then go to Europe for the year, but I resolved to make the most of the situation.

I had been in only intermittent contact with Todd, but since he had promised completion, there was nothing to worry about. There were other things to worry about.

When we arrived on Deer Isle we were in a state of excitement to really see the nearly completed house and begin to furnish it. We drove across the now familiar bridge—up, up, up, and over—and snaked onto the causeway. The tide was high; it was a beautiful, crystalline day. Turning onto our road we rolled down our windows and smelled the sweet forest air. The road now had a name and a street sign, "Margalo Lane," after the bird who saved Stuart Little's life, and flew away to the north from New York—the bird Stuart fell in love with and pursued into the countryside in his tiny automobile.

Parking on the turnaround, I looked up at the house. Most of the scaffolding had been taken down, and the house looked more or less complete. There were three or four cars and trucks parked on the packed gravel that went right up to the front of the house. There was still much work to be done to get the house to settle properly into the landscape and to heal the damage that had been done to make it possible to build, but this site repair work and landscaping could come in time. Once we were settled we could figure it all out.

Out of the car we stretched and breathed deeply. It was nice to be finally out of the car after two days on the road, and the weather was beautiful. We walked slowly up the approach road to the house, past the trucks, the port-o-let, and the dumpster.

Between the gravel and the deck there was nearly two feet of grade difference that would eventually be traversed with a wood ramp that would be integrated with the landscape. This had to wait for the completion of the rest of the house, and the removal of a certain amount of the temporary gravel in front of it. I wanted the ramp to land properly—it needed to feel like it returned to bedrock ledge—and this would take some careful investigation and design.

There was a single high temporary step at the opening that let onto the deck. The deck was new and beautiful; the smell of cedar was strong. Although there were a few shingles missing in the front porch area, it was mostly finished. The porch ceiling lights were not yet installed. I stepped up onto the front porch. The arc on the right that looked out to the woods and the water was now complete. The edge was flawless, and the shape perfect. This did not prepare me for what I was about to discover.

There was no handle on the front door, just a piece of plastic strapping threaded through where the spindle should go. Looking in, I could see that the floors were still covered in brown paper. Finished plywood panels covered only about the first half of the ceiling. The walls were still unfinished. There was a large stack of finished plywood in the middle of the living room floor. There were tools and equipment everywhere—the house was very far from finished, despite Todd's promises. Still, denial is a powerful, involuntary emotional response.

Upstairs the situation was no different. The finished plywood work was ongoing, proceeding from the guestroom at the far end and working toward our bedroom at the top of the stairs. The guest room, bunkroom, and bathrooms were nearly complete. The master bedroom was now the main staging area for cutting panels.

Construction sites have a tendency to stop when owners show up. I know this from the labor side of things. Sometimes it is close to break-time anyway, or maybe some noisy operation needs to pause so people can talk and listen. Everyone wants to know if the owner is pleased with the job or if some drama will ensue. This time was no different. Inside, I was dying with disappointment. Outside, however, I was in an information-gathering mode. After initial greetings, figuring out who was in charge, I started asking how it was going, what was happening, and what was next. Todd was nowhere to be found. I began to wonder if he was avoiding me. He would turn up later at the inn where we planned to stay the first night. He was nonplussed, surprised that I was upset that the house wasn't complete. He had completely forgotten the promise that the house would be finished.

Over the next couple of hours Peggy and I settled into the stress and disappointment of the situation. Perhaps if only I had not been so trusting, or believed Todd's story, perhaps if I had applied pressure, maybe then things would have turned out differently. But this was the situation, and nothing was going to change that. It soon became clear enough—hope against hope—that we would not be able to get into the house at all that summer. Instead, we would stay in rentals for a few weeks before we had to pack up and head off to our work in Luxembourg.

I made a list of all of the things left to do on the house: plywood panels, cabinets, toilets and sinks, medicine cabinets, electrical outlets and fixtures, shelves, doors—all needed to be installed. It was a substantial list. But there was a silver lining. There were some things that I could do and wanted to do myself. By doing them we could save some money, and I could be fully responsible for and more deeply involved with the result. I would know the house more intimately than by leaving everything to others.

There were two crews installing plywood, one upstairs, and one downstairs. After I exhorted Todd to get the job done, he hired an additional carpenter to work on door installation. Hank Whitsett came in to install sliding doors and a wood valance that ran the length of the upstairs hall. As soon as it would be practical, Bill Turner would come in to do the stair rail. I would build shelves and install hardware.

Each morning I'd wake up early, put on my blue jeans, and tiptoe out of the bedroom, make coffee, and make the three-mile drive to the house. Although I had spent a year building furniture at Huston & Company, and many summers working construction during college, I felt somewhat out of my element. Perhaps I was overly sensitive to the situation because not only was I the owner and therefore the ultimate boss, I was also the architect and a professor besides. There are so many carpenter and builder stories in which the architect is made to look the fool . . . the things we fuss over

. . . the things we do not actually know how to do . . . the degree to which we are impractical. I have heard these stories since I was seventeen years old working as a laborer and a carpenter's helper and a superintendent's assistant on union and non-union jobs. Union carpenters called me "College" for an entire summer—as in "college kid," an apparently alien species. The cat and dog stories have an element of truth to them, but they also miss an essential point, and that is the degree to which both design and workmanship are necessary for excellent building.

⧖

Even in workmanship there is design. There are decisions, separate from the decisions that architects make, that workmen are often called upon to make. This is why the tiresome antipathy between those who draw and those who build is detrimental to good building.

Details and craft are dependent upon one another. If details give meaning to architecture, and detailing is about proximity and distance, as Ford argues, then craft puts conviction behind meaning and ensures that what is seen up close accords favorably with what is seen from afar.

David Pye, the woodworker and theorist of craft, wrote *The Nature and Art of Workmanship* at a time and place (post WWII England) in which he witnessed the apparent loss of the quality of craft in the world around him due to an increasing quantity of mass-manufactured goods. The book was Pye's attempt to understand and accommodate this change. He distinguished between the "workmanship of certainty," and the "workmanship of risk," but these were far from neat categories. Pye pointed out that the craftsman always seeks to minimize risk through templates, jigs, machines, and tools. Far from being sides to be embraced or rejected in a polemic, the two kinds of workmanship are both legitimate ways of making, if thoughtfully employed by designer and craftsman.

In *The Thinking Hand: Existential and Embodied Wisdom in Architecture*, the follow-up to *The Eyes of the Skin*, Pallasmaa briefly takes up Pye's ideas about workmanship of certainty and workmanship of risk in order to make a point about architectural practice. Pallasmaa argues for more play, for less use and re-use of standard and tested solutions and methods, and for more adventurous experimentation with structure, form, material, and detail. He describes and quotes Aalto on his manner of work, pointing out the relationship between the focused consciousness and the relaxed consciousness that confirms "... the non-linearity of the design process and the essential aspect of zooming back and forth between various scales and aspects of a project ..."

Pallasmaa's call for play is a basic claim about the design process—a plea to designers for freedom and imagination, a plea made by numerous other writers—but in issuing such a plea he underlines a critical point about the difference between designing and making. Designing is the arena within which it is always possible to play longer—the stakes remain very low: the crew has not yet been mobilized, the material remains in the ground. The designer can afford to play, whereas for the craftsman and maker and builder there is inevitably the need to minimize, or at least greatly reduce, uncertainty and risk. Perhaps the most useful understanding a designer might draw from Pye's argument about workmanship is the distinction between designing and crafting. Designing is an arena in which risk is low, play can be never-ending, voluminous, and free ranging. Its objective is to get to the point where it is possible to anticipate the use of jigs and tools, to imagine the degree of certainty and risk, and thus to be able to proceed. If craft can be a risky proposition, then designing is the art of consuming some or all of that risk.

Marco Frascari, in *Eleven Exercises in the Art of Architectural Drawing: Slow Food for the Architect's Imagination,* sees drawing as the locus of design. Play, accident, and discovery may be fostered through approaches to drawing that set up analogies, promote metaphor, and expand the senses. Frascari wants drawings that are made. The designer—the one who marks out with the hand—should taste the drawings that she makes, and feel the way the parts go together, perhaps with eyes closed. The designer should get lost in the drawings in order to find something unexpected.

This partly explains why design is such a time-consuming activity. The designer must play to invent, but also play into every dead-end and blind alley while uprooting every threat. It is creative and defensive activity at the same time. It can seem to involve nothing but insurmountable problems, and then it can feel like a state of flow in which solid conclusions seem to arise all by themselves. This is why, in designing the shear wall, it seemed in the end to have designed itself. And why, walking the site, trying to find the proper relationship of building to land, of threshold and of idea, just starting seemed to take a very long time and then, as if in a flood, the essential outline of the work fell rapidly into place. In other words, there is much about the activity of design that would appear from the outside as non-activity.

⧗

According to David Pye, "design proposes[,] workmanship disposes[,]," meaning that the person who draws, shapes the work and craft can either make or wreck it. We depend upon the skill, the finesse, and the aesthetic judgments of others, as well as their integrity. Design and building are inherently social activities; people design and build in groups or teams, and there are numerous peripatetic and temporarily involved actors. In building the house, the basic strategy with respect to craft and the quality of construction overall was to rely upon some of the men and women of Deer Isle: craftspeople who depend upon building construction as one aspect of their livelihood. It was also to ask some basic questions, such as: How will the thing be done? What is the nature of the material? Who will do the work? What is the nature of the person's skill? A careful effort was made to match the right person with the work, and for this reason the quality of craft throughout is very high.

While there are aspects of the house that required considerable levels of skill (the plywood interior, the custom cabinetry, and the custom furniture, for example) relatively little workmanship of risk was required. As Pye points out, jigs, templates, and other "shape determining systems," reduce risk. The difference between the workmanship of certainty and the workmanship of risk has to do with whether the workman is aiming toward a predetermined result—a level of quality, a specific shape—that can't be changed once the work begins.

The house contains examples of woodworking craft representative of the control that David Pye characterizes as ranging from certainty to risk. One of these examples is the plywood paneling, a mass manufactured material, which you would think embodies the workmanship of certainty, but which must be finished, cut, and made to conform closely to the vagaries of a rough lumber building frame. There are carpenters who, despite the apparent certainty of the system, could have screwed up the plywood installation through carelessness and error.

At the other end of the spectrum, embodying the spirit of the workmanship of risk, are the several pieces of furniture made of red oak logs that were salvaged from the road building operation. These involve the workmanship of risk in two ways: first, by being made of boards shop dried next to a woodstove in winter, they are more alive and reactive than plywood or kiln dried material, and second, by being hand worked with a plane rather than worked by machine, they rely on and record every rough and free stroke from the craftsman's hand.

Experienced carpenters know that good craftsmanship results from knowing how to hide or blend inconsistencies inherent in the work. Relying on the human capacity to see the nearly level as level or the barely tapered as straight, the carpenter knows where the viewer's attention will fall. The quality and fitness of joints is often more important than consistency of dimension or even, in some cases, whether the work is square, straight, or level. The on-site carpenter therefore often deals with non-conformities that would frustrate the cabinetmaker who works with the precision of a machinist.

Jim Cust and Tristan Soloman finished the interior of the house using some eighty sheets of half-inch birch plywood held in place with square-drive deck screws that, because the heads were small and coated, could be both visible and unobtrusive. In this instance selection of material, the craftsman's task, was also important. The most highly figured sheets with dark heartwood were sorted out for use in the smaller sleeping rooms upstairs while the more consistent light sapwood sheets were reserved for the larger "public" rooms downstairs. The process of measuring, cutting, and installing the plywood required methodical patience and the use of a plunge cut track saw that could cut precisely without edge splintering. All of the sheets were given a single coat of water-based matte polyurethane prior to being cut and installed and an additional final coat after installation. As a question of workmanship, this particular work required care, dedication, and perseverance, even in the use of the track and other jigs. The carpenters sorted the panels into those with relatively clear and uniform grain and those with the darker figure of sapwood. They gave these patterns amusing names: "sea-dragon," "batwing," and "storm cloud," aware of how the patterns might be played with and remembered while resting on a beautiful afternoon.

As David Pye points out, whether or not a particular kind of work uses a jig to guide or enforce a pattern is really beside the point with respect to workmanship. After all, even the simplest tools are designed and handled in such a way as to improve their guidance. Nor is good workmanship simply a matter of not spoiling the work when one is engaged in the workmanship of risk. Rather, good workmanship results in a special quality that involves "depth, subtlety, overtones, variegation, [or] diversity." The workman, through the choices and selections he makes, the way he uses his jigs and tools, and the degree to which he is free or rough with the work he makes, adds to or detracts from the intentions of the designer for the design. Selecting "sea-dragon" figured plywood for the wall above the master bed, ensuring the panels are laid out and cut accurately, and ensuring proper fastening with care—work of the head, heart, and hand—are all necessary for good workmanship.

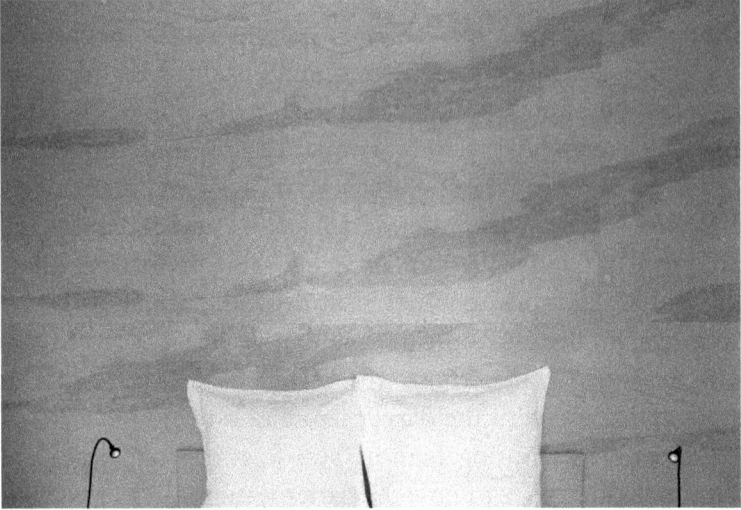

*. . . how the patterns might be played with and remembered
while resting during a beautiful afternoon . . .*

My house was not a particularly expensive house—we had a budget with constraints, and we struggled to remain within it. At one point in the process I had to look at every line item and ask what was essential, and what could be cut. I had three options for storage in the upstairs rooms, from greatest to least expense: casework, built-in closets with doors, or open shelves. One substantial cut would be the casework in the upstairs rooms. I would not usually choose open shelves for a house that a family lived in year round, especially for someone else, but for a summer house for myself this would not only be the least expensive option, it would also be in the spirit of summer living. One lives very casually and temporally—and temporarily—in a summer house. My task, therefore, as carpenter on my own project, was to build shelves.

A good shelf of wood or plywood is sufficiently thick, or its thickness is augmented with a cleat and/or a wide facing edge, so that it spans without sagging. An architect should know how far it is possible to span with a given thickness for a given load. An architect should also know the implications of using various materials and strategies for any given shelving situation. This is not special knowledge, it's fundamental. A craftsman, when tasked by an architect with building shelves, should also know these things, and bring to the task a level of decision-making that makes of the work something more than the minimum that has been asked for—this is the essence of good workmanship.

The shelves were made of ¾" birch plywood. In places they were used for books, and they had a relatively short span—well under three feet—so they needed a ¾" x 1 ½" piece of solid birch on the front edge. In other places they carried towels and linens, so they were very deep, and they also spanned more than three feet, so they required a cleat in addition to the solid leading edge. Now what the architect's drawings do not tell you are several things: how to fasten the solid leading edge to the plywood; whether or not to sand any part of that edge; if gluing, screwing, and plugging that edge, where exactly to do so; how to select the grain of the leading edge; how to size, position, and fasten the cleats. And there is more: how to align the top of the leading edge with the plywood so that the faintest sanding will bring the two into a perfect plane; how to select and place plugs so that the grain blends nicely; how to cut the leading edge a little long so that it fits snugly (but not too snugly) against whatever it is up against; how to trim plugs so they are easily sanded. Practicing craft well makes for a good detail—not a meaningful detail, but one that contributes to the overall work. A contributive detail is as important for what it does not do—call attention to itself through bad workmanship, for example—as for what it does, which is to allow the building to work.

I learned woodworking from my friend Bill Huston during a year I found myself suddenly unemployed in Portland in a collapsed real estate economy. Architects with far more experience were also out of work, and there was no sign of immediate improvement. Bill and I had worked together at Thos. Moser Cabinetmakers (I had moved to Portland after graduate school to go to work for Tom) and we were good friends. In my unemployment, Bill offered to train me and put me to work; neither of us intended or expected it to be a permanent arrangement. I saw it as an opportunity to advance my practical architectural knowledge and skill. I ended up learning a lot about the range of decisions that one must make that contribute to workmanship in highly crafted objects.

Bill came from a family with a strong history of entrepreneurship and making things. His grandfather established the Xenia (Ohio) Foundry and Machine Company in 1920, a company that is still run by members of the family, but as a young man Bill made a decision to follow a career path in woodworking. He sought training abroad in the 1970s, living and working for two years in Blaker, Norway. He moved to Maine and worked for twelve years for Thos. Moser Cabinetmakers. He then opened his own shop, Huston & Company, in 1988, first in Poland Spring, Maine, and later in Kennebunkport. In Bill I found a kindred spirit, an honest, thoughtful, and gentle man, and working with him I felt reconnected with my own Scandinavian-carpenter heritage.

The craftsmen who built the house made thoughtful craft choices throughout, but a particular example demonstrates how one of Huston & Company's decisions contributed to the design. Huston & Company built the six cabinets behind the kitchen counter (as well as the rest of the kitchen). These cabinets form a wall twelve feet long and seven feet high. In my drawings I called for an overlay door in maple veneer plywood with hardwood edges and a simple stainless steel pull. The task for Huston & Company was straightforward: build strong cases, choose heavy-duty hinges, and select good material for the doors. Bill ordered three four-by-eight sheets of book-matched maple veneer plywood from his regular supplier and divided each of these for the doors.

When I arrived at the unfinished house the six tall cabinets were standing there, awaiting finished walls to which to attach them. Soon, the walls were closed in, and Hank was given the task to do the installation. He needed to know the exact placement. I checked the existing dimension of the wall against my drawing, and consulted the refrigerator installation manual for the refrigerator and clearance dimensions. My intention had always been to create a loose, rather than a rigid relationship between the bank of cabinets and the controlling order of the house, and to treat the refrigerator as a freestanding object, rather than one that was built-in. In my mind this was a radical idea in a world that carries the gestalt of the built-in kitchen to obsessive extremes—it seemed a fitting approach that acknowledged the camp as precedent. In addition, the bank of cabinets would come only as close to the steel shear wall as felt comfortable. Floating near one another, their connection not resolved, space would be the third term between them.

With a few quick calculations I gave Hank the starting point for the bank of cabinets, and within a couple of hours he had them bolted securely to the wall. I know this because I was summoned from my shelf-making work upstairs; I was wanted in the kitchen. Downstairs, I found that Hank and Mike had attempted to slide the refrigerator into position and found that it would not fit; all work had momentarily stopped so that whatever drama might unfold might be observed. All eyes were on me. There was a good chance I was being cast in the role of the Foolish Architect, and clearly I had made a mistake with actual consequences. I looked at the refrigerator literature and soon understood the mistake I had made by misreading the dimensions. The cabinets would have to be unbolted, moved a few inches to the right, and fastened again. Not a problem, I thought, pleased that I had designed the wall with a flexible positioning scheme.

The boards used for the veneer of the tall kitchen cabinets contained a couple of small tight knots which, because of the book matching, repeat every eight inches or so across the wall of doors. It is a subtle repetition of sixes that introduces another level of order to the design. It is probably not a detail that most people would notice, but it is there nonetheless, reiterating the variably dimensioned numerology that begins at the largest level of organization of the house and continues into details: six structural modules at twelve feet each, six cabinets at two feet each, six glass half-spheres and lamps overhead, etc.

This enhancement of the design was in part accidental, a result of the particular panels that happened to be shipped when Huston & Company ordered them, but it was also intentional, the result of the judgment that is an aspect of the cabinetmaker's art. In fact, when I remarked to Bill that I thought the matching on the face of the doors was particularly nice, he told me a story about how the three panels had almost been separated in the shop and one used for a different purpose. He had rescued them from this fate only by chance and at the last possible moment.

I find it interesting that I read into the detail of the panels with knowledge of the overall design of the building that other people might not have, or might not even care about. You could say that the detail is simply too subtle to matter, but I notice it, and it either has meaning, or I imbue it with meaning. Bill probably doesn't care so much about how the pattern of the repetition of the tiny knots connects with the larger order of the building, but he certainly cares, as a craftsman of long experience, that the pattern works well within the field of six doors. He cares, in a detached way, about the overall quality of his work in relation to all other work that he has done. Another person, neither architect nor craftsman, might not care, or have a thought or judgment, about this detail of design, but I would hope that they might be unconsciously affected, or remain open-minded enough to begin to become conscious that something more is going on beyond the surface appearance. Far too many people are governed by what is marketed to them, by what they see on HGTV, and by the dismal offerings at the big box stores to ever really be able to develop ways of seeing for themselves.

⌛

This is my favorite story from my weeks of working on the house: Sarah Lawson, Todd's wife, who does all of the painting on their projects, has mentioned that she has hired an additional person to come in and help her with applying the finish to the plywood, doors, and window frames. It is early morning, and I am upstairs in the bedroom working over my sawhorses, gluing and screwing leading edges to shelves. Several people are coming through the house, walking down the hall: Walter, Hank, Todd, then Sarah and a woman I do not recognize. They pause. The woman is looking around, then she turns to Sarah and says, "This is the *strangest* house I have *ever* seen."

I did not look up from my work. In a way it felt like a compliment.

Later, Sarah told me that she had told the woman that she wouldn't be needed for the job. Sarah went out of her way to tell me this. She must have thought that I would be offended or somehow hurt by the comment. I was so very far from offended; I was amused. But sad, too—I imagined the woman had no capacity to see anything other than a familiar form—a ranch or a cape or some other common type—as a house.

⧗

We were disappointed to not be able to move into the house that summer, but I felt it was a gift to be able to participate in building it. We enjoyed our few weeks on Deer Isle, then drove to Boston and flew to Luxembourg for the year. Luxembourg brought its own rewards, including a wonderful international school experience for Callie and Hugh, trips to experience great art and architecture, students who were excited about what they were learning, tens of thousands of photographs, and an expat exercise in stripped-down apartment living with basic furnishings from Ikea. The following summer, our time and travels in Europe over, we were at last able to move into the house and begin the process of furnishing it.

⧗

While David Pye distinguishes between workmanship of certainty and workmanship of risk, he also recognizes other forms of judgment as essential to craft quality. Workmanship adds to or detracts from the work. In woodworking, selection of materials, and choosing particular pieces of stock for specific places in the work, matter to the result. Selection, material qualities, accident, time, and tooling processes can all contribute positively to the result, often by lending variety, and these are sometimes within the control, and always within the purview of the craftsman.

Another craftsman who contributed greatly to the project is a man by the name of Bill Turner, a back-to-the-lander, farmer, and woodworker who trained at the North Bennet Street School in Boston. Bill and Julie Turner established Spruce Hill Farm in the seventies, raising their two daughters in the spirit of hands-on self-education and self-reliance. As members of a strong community, the Turners raise goats for their own meat and operate a farm stand to sell their excellent goat cheeses. During the summer they produce crops for canning and immediate consumption. They raise chickens for meat and eggs as well. One day Bill came to the house to discuss a new project I had in mind.

We were designing and building a bench for the living room. The idea had alighted one day when Peggy and I were talking about the back of the sofa. This sounds stupid, but it's not, really, that is, if you consider solving interior design problems at all important. The back of the sofa will fold down to allow it to become a bed, so there is a chrome and steel frame that you see from the back, and it is ungainly. We had always imagined that there would be some kind of table or other object behind the sofa that would be both useful and beautiful, and which would also partially cover and mitigate the awkwardness of the sofa's frame. The idea that struck was a vision for a bench made from some of the reclaimed oak. It would be massive and somewhat primitive. The oak, as it air-dried, would likely check, maybe twist and split.

I had determined that it should be six feet long and, to serve as a bench, it needed to be seventeen to eighteen inches high and at least twelve inches wide. At first I had assumed that we would try to cut a twelve by twelve timber, and place it on a pair of six by six blocks, but reality soon dictated otherwise. The logs would not yield timber that large. We thought about stacking the pieces one on top of each other, but also about standing them side by side and tying them together. This is the approach I favored from the beginning, because I knew that it represented the normal structural action of the beam, and also because I intuitively knew that there ought to be an air space between the beams, since air-drying such a large beam would be a challenge anyway. I said something to Bill about this airspace and spacing the beams an inch apart. He looked at me with some curiosity and then suggested that we might use a butterfly joint, which he began to draw with a pencil on the end of a log.

"Design composes, workmanship disposes," suggests that there is a dividing line between designing and making, but this is a blurred line. For the furniture craftsman and designer the line barely exists, as what is so crucial to the development of the work is an iterative process whereby each partial attempt at finishing informs the work of producing a viable design drawing. In the case of the twinned timber bench the work was so simple, and the requirements so basic, that very little in the way of iteration was needed. Still, the collaboration between designer and craftsman reveals how the knowledge of each other's working methods is critical to the work.

Because the twinned timber bench was meant to solve a particular problem, this could be articulated in terms of dimensions that turned out to reflect larger interests. In the process of sketching and discussing, "a bench about six feet long," became a bench precisely six feet long, fifteen inches high, and about twelve inches wide. It soon became important whether it would be possible to cut six by twelve timbers from the logs we had. If so, then the bench could be composed of a pair of timbers separated by a gap, supported by two blocks that were themselves six inches by six inches square. All of this was recorded in a drawing made roughly to scale and even though the decisions were provisional, dependent upon what might happen at the sawmill, the drawing sparked three key suggestions from Bill.

First, this would be very much like the kind of working in timber that might have been undertaken for the construction of a house or barn frame and, since the timber would be worked green, twisting, checking, and splitting should be expected. Still, to minimize the extent and impact of this uncontrolled drying, Bill could use the Japanese technique of cutting a deep slot in the hidden, long face of each timber where they came together. This would be entirely experimental, and would not guarantee that checks and splits would not occur, but it might minimize them.

The second suggestion concerned the butterfly joint: the method of connecting the twinned timbers, which needed to be both held together and held apart at the same time. The butterfly shaped block of wood, dovetailed into each timber, would serve the purpose, ornament the work, and celebrate the traditions of the wood-joiner's art. All that remained was to proportion it correctly.

The third suggestion would have no visible aesthetic impact, as it concerned the method of attaching the support blocks to the timbers and would therefore be hidden, but as any carpenter or woodworker knows, as a spiritual imperative the hidden work must be as sound as that which is visible, even if executed roughly. Bill suggested he use a wedge and pintle connection: a dowel of oak or ash, with a wedge in each end, that when driven home expands the diameter of the dowel into the wall of the boring in which it is driven, resulting in a tight and permanent connection without the introduction of a metal screw or bolt.

One day after our preliminary designing was finished I went to the Turner's farm and walked up the hill to the sawmill that Bill had rebuilt from the essential mechanical parts of an old sawmill from Isle au Haut. The sawmill dates from the nineteen twenties and in an instance of coincidence or karmic destiny, it bears a label as a patented "Turner" sawmill. Bill sees it very much as a community service to operate it. It embodies local knowledge tied to local resources, used as it is to work the island spruce, red oak, and other woods. To saw a log you slide or roll it into position on a carriage and lock it down with a pair of dogs. The mechanism at each end of the log can then be adjusted to position the log for sawing. A cable pulls the carriage, which rests on a pair of iron tracks, to draw the log into the three-foot diameter blade. It is simple, but effective.

Our task was to take two of the red oak logs that were salvaged from the land when the road was put in and cut them into six by twelve beams if they would yield pieces that large. My job was mainly to watch and occasionally to pull slabs or boards off the roller slide after they were cut off the log. In a few minutes Bill had cut one of the six by twelve beams and, after a trip to the field to pick up a second log, he cut the second beam. The second one turned out to be even better than the first, with good clear grain, no defects, and only the slightest edge of sapwood.

As it turned out, the milling process confirmed that it was possible to produce two six-inch by twelve-inch timbers from the salvaged logs. Not massive, and cut straight from the heart of the log, but adequate for the purpose. Bill

executed the bench as designed. He used a scrub plane to remove the saw marks from the exposed surface. The piece was
oiled and re-oiled, allowed to dry further in situ, and finally
waxed. It has checked and split, minimally, and will continue
to develop patina and character as it ages. A delight to all the
senses, if protected, the bench will last for several hundred
years before the wood begins to break down.

. . . simple, but effective . . .

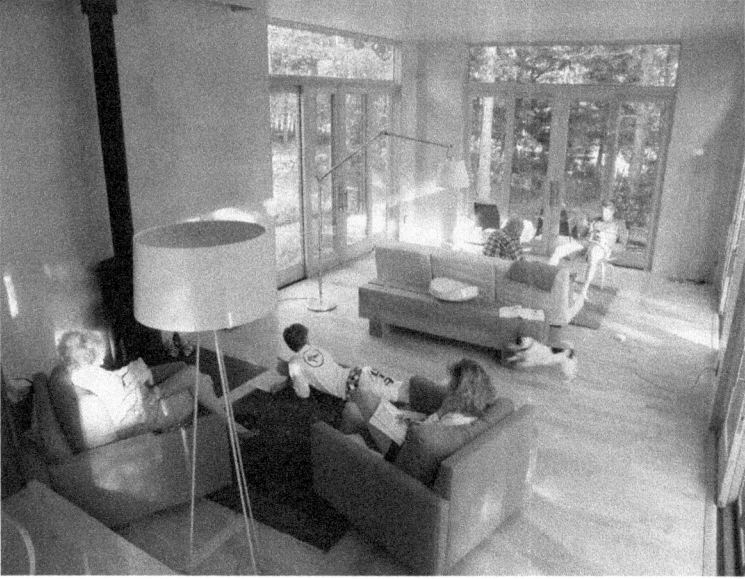

. . . if protected, the bench will last for several hundred years before the wood begins to break down . . .

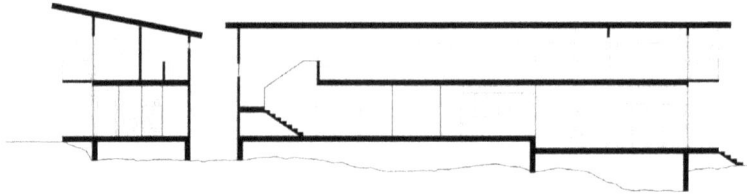

1 ENTRY

2 KITCHEN / DINING

3 LIVING

4 MUD ROOM

5 BEDROOM

6 BUNK ROOM

7 OFFICE / BEDROOM

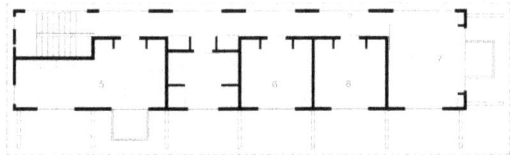

SECOND FLOOR

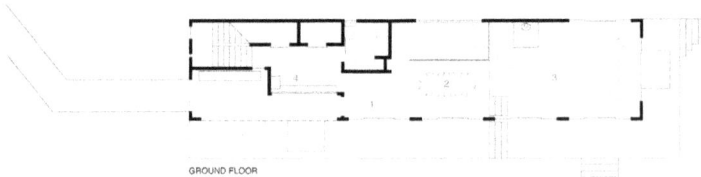

GROUND FLOOR

plan and section diagrams

6. Photographs

Photographs tend to annihilate the multisensory experience in the present that is architecture's value, if not its essence. As compositional constructs, and as objects in their own right, photographs preference the visual sense above all others. In this way photographs often parallel the historical hierarchy of the senses.

But many photographs speak of senses beyond the purely visual. A photograph can suggest moment and time in light and shadow, or mood of weather or viewer. A photograph can make you feel like you are there, or impossibly far away, all alone or all together.

The camera edits, amplifying the unwanted, drawing an inflexible rectangular frame of given proportion, thereby cutting a sharp hole in the world and flattening what is round, and so the photographer must edit too by framing, selecting, composing, angling, eliminating.

Truly expert, technically accomplished, architectural photographers can make the architectural subject seem somehow more visually thrilling than it would ever feel in actual experience. To do this, at least with most interior shots, the photographer must bring a battery of equipment. Carrying and setting up the equipment, as a site assistant for one such commercial photographer before college, I sharpened the compositional sensibility that my parent's had given me through art, and I learned just how much exhausting and painstaking work, just how much artifice goes into the exaggerating of visual reality for exciting effect in the image.

The rap on the photography of architecture is not especially positive. Photographs are spectacle. They are product-driven, and they mislead or tell outright lies. In consumer culture, architecture is simply not legitimate until it makes it into the glossy magazine via the dazzling photograph—or so the culture seems to say. I have heard that some architects design with specific future camera angles and positions in mind, although I find this hard to believe.

On the plus side, slick photographs do not easily fool good architects. They know how to read carefully, combining photographic views with plan and section diagrams, to develop a reasonably accurate sense of a building.

A professional architectural photographer, like a photographic artist, is always bringing a point of view to the subject. Who knows what combination of birth and upbringing, training and experience ultimately shapes and affirms the photographer's point of view. For the expert photographer, as for any of us, looking through the camera is looking in a particular way.

We might begin to think of the relationship between photography and architecture differently if more architects made and shared their own photographs. In this chapter, I've done exactly that, albeit with nothing more to aid the endeavor than natural light and a decent digital camera (without parallax correction).

A photograph tells you something about the way the photographer sees, so when an architect takes photographs of something he has designed he is showing you in at least two different ways how he sees: first in the thing pictured (provided the picture is not misleading), and second in the capturing of the composition itself. A third revelation might be of the moment: a capturing of mood, of light, of action, of weather.

Photographs can also encapsulate ideas, whether broad, abstract, specific, or concrete. A photograph of a work of architecture might reveal a relationship to landscape, a structural idea, a compositional gesture, the nature of enclosure, a delicate detail, a motif, a texture, a threshold, rhythms and repetitions, material qualities, a function, an affordance, the light on surfaces, a metaphor, an allusion, or the relative position of the work in the larger order of the universe. In this sense photographs can reveal ideas, and thus shape perceptions, that might otherwise remain half-hidden.

Architectural photography has tended to push the lens into the world in front of a solitary viewer, leaving other people out of the scene. This tendency has the advantage of emphasizing inanimate surroundings, which sometimes have a hard time competing for attention against other human beings. The disadvantage, of course, is a potentially less compelling image, or an image with missing information such as scale, or how a space might be used.

The photographs included here are mostly devoid of human figures, mostly following the conventions of architectural photography, and meant to deliver facts, compositional knowledge, and reveal ways of seeing. Still, photographs are no substitute for in-the-moment experience of the actual thing.

The shed, along with the north wall of the house, frames a kind of entry forecourt, and the opposing angles gesture around a center. The textural differences reiterate the idea that the composition is both loose and formal.

The entry walkway takes off from an exposed piece of pink granite ledge, surrounded by native ferns and wild blueberry.

When you have reached this point you have walked a hundred or more paces from the gravel road in the woods. You have begun to slow down. You listen. It is quiet. You embark onto the walkway as if from shore onto a dock. You begin to enter the house as if it is a boat ready to detach itself from the land.

The north elevation, in shadow most of the time, except in late afternoon in summer, is punctured with squares and rectangles arrayed like elements in a constellation. I was thinking of the dog's view from the stair landing, people's views from the square windows, reflected light, the composition and its proportions, and Ronchamp.

Cedar shingles and boards have a venerable history in coastal Maine. Though a practical choice, they will not last forever. They feel warm, friendly, human.

The cedar deck begins close to the granite dome, where the design of the house began. It floats above, as a boat might. From here one can have a vantage point, and look out, while feeling safe, remembering only the earth will last, and even that not unchanged.

It's a cliché: two old people looking west. There they sit, hammer and screwdriver, together in the toolbox of communication, to quote Terry Pratchett, communicating. Clichés are clichés because they are true.

This view looks north. The house, as high as the tree line, springs from the great body of land and begins to drift off. The balcony hangs precariously, an airy perch from which to survey sea and land.

The front door is sheltered, as all front doors should be. Here at the critical threshold there is some emphasis on the vertical gesture before opening to a horizontal world.

It is a warm world, wrapped entirely in birch and maple.
The steel feels like worn leather. The first heart of this world
is the dining table, from which all things are done.

The center of this world is a red oak bowl turned by Jorge Castenada, a lifelong Deer Isle resident. Jorge told me, and you can see it in the wobble of the rim, that the green wood used to turn the bowl released its tension all at once, nearly at the moment that the turning was finished, so Jorge stopped. It looks like it is still spinning, a fitting center for an array of rectangles and squares defining rooms.

The hearth, the ancestral center of home, is fittingly square.
In June, when the cold drizzle falls outside in the fog, a fire
keeps the spirit dancing, while at other times the hearth is
enlivened by sunlight. Cool or warm it is never dead.

The term "atmosphere," applied to architecture, refers to
multisensory perception in a particular moment in space. This
room, the main living room of the house, possesses atmosphere
because of its particular relationship to the surrounding
forest. In this room one is also in the forest, participating
in its light, sound, and weather, operating its doors.

What a strange view. Who looks into the ceiling corners of rooms? A ten-foot ceiling floats, thirteen feet above the ground, in the air along the trajectory to treetops.

The house possesses a numerology, often of sixes.
Though repetitive, it is not rigid. It plays against
parallelism, within which spins the round.

Real life, of course, is often a mess, and so it is good to hide behind a high plane-wing of steel when cooking and cleaning up, the better to corral pots and dirty dishes and vouchsafe those fortunate enough to possess a moment of leisure, untroubled by flying insects.

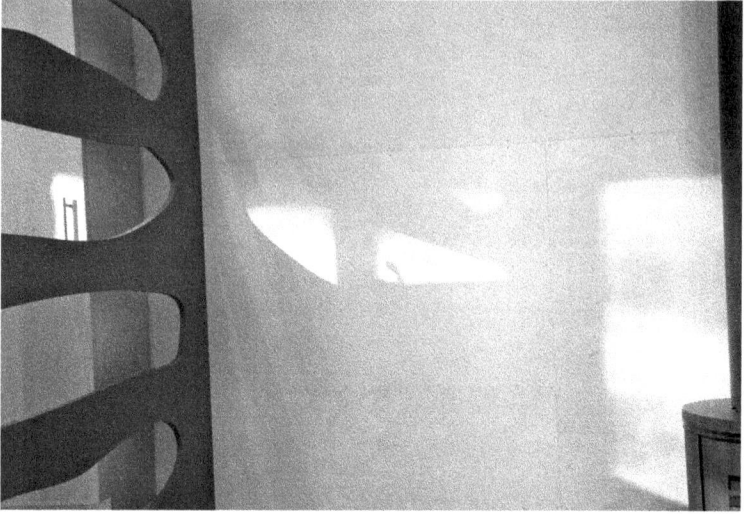

*Aiming a camera one can see things not likely to
be seen again in that one particular way.*

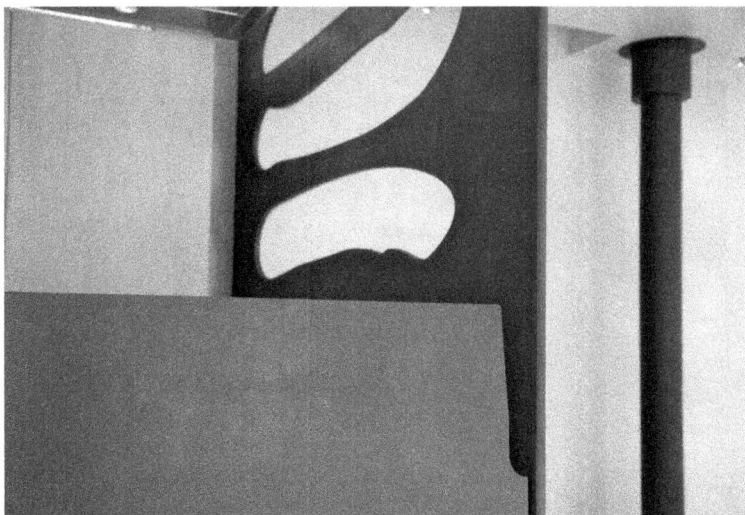

I like a photograph that breaks down the world into a composition of rectangles. It is a prison and a gift.

Like an old tool, the steel plate of the wall that separates the kitchen from the dining area swings down into a half-circle, an arc inviting the tip of the finger and the eye.

There is a lot going on in the mudroom, it hardly ever looks this clean. The mirror above the hanging cabinet is a hundred years old. It masquerades as a window and plays just as the horizontal slot plays and the little rectangular hole on the landing plays, all letting in light and speaking to each other of their differences.

The stair hall is a heavenly space, lit from the east,
pierced to the north, and hung with celestial orbs.
Its beauty is entirely unnecessary and essential.

This photograph suggests the glass sphere on the right is the source of light, a misleading though not unpleasant notion. It feels good to stand on the landing and look out the square window, especially when it rains. One is on the way somewhere, and going nowhere at all.

In the morning the long hallway explodes with reflected sunlight. The stainless steel flue from the fireplace below marks the hall near the end like a mile-marker.

*I love the complexity of this picture. It's a simple
space, transformed by late afternoon light, both
intimate and generous, holding and releasing.*

The viewer, on the balcony at the south end of the house where the roof overhang frames the forest, is halfway up in the trees. It's a secret aerie, especially for the solitary guest.

The balcony hangs from the roof on a pair of rods, simply detailed as on a boat or a suspension bridge, safe but with a lively bounce.

Built above ledge, among boulders and stones, the
natural order of the landscape prevails. The hay
scented ferns return fiercely each spring.

This picture is about one of the main ideas of the building: a pavilion in a forest. The building is all verticality and angled limbs and canopy. Among these tree's denizens are red squirrels, goldfinches, pileated woodpeckers, downy woodpeckers, flickers, ruby-throated hummingbirds, owls, and raccoons—and a pavilion makes a fine place from which to enjoy their doings.

The east wall of the house, cast in dappled morning light, demurs to distant neighbors. Mostly closed in, there are slit windows for seeing out and small awning windows for natural ventilation. Though conceived to remain mostly hidden from view, it nevertheless presents a strong face.

Flooded with light through its layered walls,
the shed is the house in miniature.

With a sliding window that looks out to the west, it is a pleasant place to work, rain or shine. It holds garden tools and kayaks, which can be slipped in through a narrow door at the south end.

Against the wall, in the drip line, butterflies and bees work ardently among the wild blueberry and sea holly, but only after the middle of July.

The steps are old slabs of Deer Isle Granite, with decades-old wheels of lichen. There, satisfaction is in soundness under foot.

Even in something like the placement of screws, as on the shed doors, proportions matter. Nothing is arbitrary. Here the designer and craftsman become one.

The outdoor shower is a broken slab of granite,
sloped to the crack to form a natural drain.

The view from the house looking toward the west and the big boulder and the five trunked oak and the water beyond. The forest is tended. It is easy to walk to the shore where there is no discernible trace of the agreeable spot where I once pitched a tent.

The swimming spot, where eight blocks of salvaged granite form stepping stones out to the big ledge. Because of the mud, its warmer here than most Maine waters, and agreeable when the sun has been warming the mud all day before the tide comes up.

The view toward Indian Carrying Place,
where the road to Haystack crosses.

Jorge Castenada's bowl on Bill Huston's table.

The table ready for dinner.

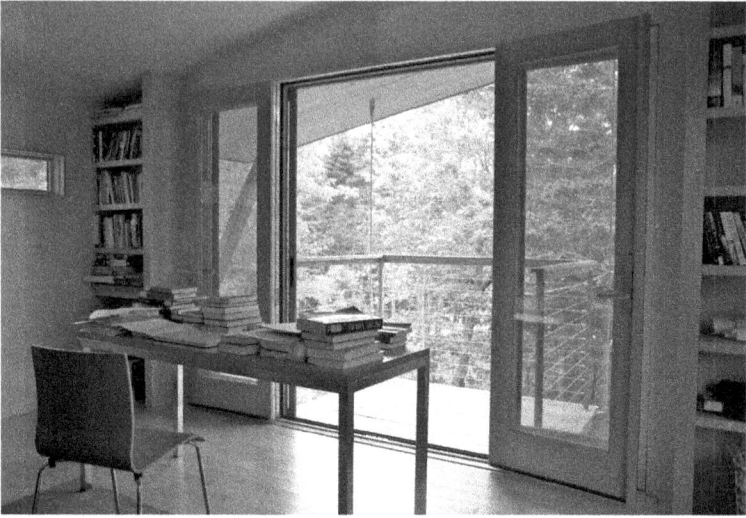

"Mindful physical presence," "direct aesthetic experience of the real," "the quality without a name," these are different ways of speaking of architectural atmosphere.

7. Atmosphere

Atmosphere is the overarching perceptual, sensory, and emotive impression of a space, setting, or social situation. It provides the unifying coherence and character for a room, space, place, and landscape, or a social encounter. It is "the common denominator", "the colouring" or "the feel" of the experiential situation. Atmosphere is a mental "thing", an experiential property or characteristic that is suspended between the object and the subject.

—Juhani Pallasmaa[7]

Sitting in the house at the dining table, I look around and drink my coffee. By the wet edge on the deck outside it

[7] Juhani Pallasmaa, "Space, Place, and Atmosphere: Peripheral Perception in Existential Experience," in Christian Borch, ed. *Architectural Atmospheres: On the Experience and Politics of Architecture*, Basel: Birkhauser, 2015, p. 20-21.

appears it rained in the night. Peggy is still asleep upstairs. Callie and Hugh are away with friends. Silence. I imagined the house that now surrounds me, and I can't see it. I look at it, out of it, inhabit its rooms, stand on its decks, walk around it on earth, stand next to its front wall, but I can't see it. Such a strange feeling, to sit here and not be able to see the house, to only be able to think about decisions about materials and arrangement, and each of its separate details. Peggy exclaims, "It's so beautiful!" but I can't see it. I long to be able to see the house from her perspective, with something like innocence or detachment, but this feels like an impossible desire.

On a different morning I am in the living room seated on the sofa facing toward the south, toward the cove. It is before six. Through the forest there are patches of lavender and rose-colored sky. Beyond a long, low, charcoal-colored table on a bright red rug, there are two molded ash plywood chairs, and beyond the spruce frames of the sliding glass doors the forest gathers gloomy shadows. The moss-covered boulders are brilliant green, even in low light. Above and through the glass the stainless steel frame of the upper balcony hangs like a halo. The way the house sits in the forest is so beautiful. This morning I can see it, appreciate it, and yet ascribe the credit for this beauty to the melancholy of the surrounding woods, to the sweetness of the mourning doves, and to the briny rivulets of alternately warm and cool air that move across the room. This beauty doesn't have anything to do with design, or anything I have done. Or so I think.

All through the process of designing and building the house there were many doubts—worries about everything, even about whether worry and doubt would negatively affect the outcome. To worry the details is very much a part of my temperament and habit. This habit is necessary to building and to architecture, to getting the details right, but it also has a tendency to take pleasure away.

But I am edging toward some small measure of contentment. Perhaps I have lived with the house long enough now. There are mistakes, but only of the most insignificant kind. I do not look and believe that some important thing should have been done differently. Fortunately, there has been no major regret.

On a different day, in another mood, I have entertained how I might have designed a part of the building differently, or even the whole of the building, but have concluded it is right the way it is. For a moment the building is exceedingly beautiful, and this pleases me, even if it has mostly to do with harnessing the already powerful attributes of the place. I succeeded in making one right thing, one beautiful thing. Still, I do not know what beauty is, or where it comes from.

⧗

Designing the house, building the house, furnishing and living in the house, taking pictures of the house, thinking about it, and writing I became aware of the term atmosphere. It must have been during our year in Europe, visiting Peter Zumthor's projects. Though I very much believe in the idea of atmospheres now, I did not know about it when designing. Then I had to rely on a different vocabulary to think about what to do.

The essence of the word atmosphere, carried in its etymology, already begins to give an indication of its significance as a concept for architecture. The seventeenth century word *atmosphaera* comes to us from Modern Latin, combined from the Greek *atmos*, "steam, vapor," plus *spharia*, "sphere." *Atmos* is from Proto-Indo-European *awet-mo-*, from root *wet-* "to blow, also "to inspire, spiritually arouse." Atmosphere is round, like our direct bodily experience of the world, and, like *aesthethis* itself, it evokes the sense of breath if not of something like a spirit. At the least, the perceiving individual breathes at atmosphere's center.

Atmosphere's spherical nature brings to mind Bachelard's roundness, but as a phenomenological-architectural concept it is also akin to what Michael Benedikt has called "direct aesthetic experience of the real," or what Christopher Alexander referred to when he evoked, "the quality without a name," which every person presumably has a strong desire both to create and to perceive, or what I once referred to in my essays on walking as *merging*, the action of perceiving atmosphere. In other words, atmosphere has gone by other names, and as an architectural concept is not so new, but it is important.

As a concept of architectural aesthetics, atmosphere is more important now than it has ever been because of the diminishment of actual architectural experiences by virtual ones. Architectural atmosphere stands in contrast to the flatness of pictures and the limited sensation of virtual experience that threatens to overrun architectural experience and take us out of place. For all of our digital extensions of perception we are, in the end, where we are, surrounded by what surrounds us, and this is the locus of atmosphere. Architectural atmosphere implies a sum that is greater than the apparent parts, a totality of interacting qualities, and multisensory perception with the perceiving individuals at the center of it all. The term atmosphere in architecture is a useful way of recognizing multisensory experience. Although senses have for a long time been reduced to only five, with vision at the apex, there are reasons to rethink this hierarchy.

Philosophers, architects, and other scholars have explored explicitly the idea of atmosphere as an aesthetic concept for a couple of decades or more. German philosopher Gernot Böhme, proceeding from his 1989 book calling for an aesthetics grounded in ecology, *Fur eine okölogische Natureästhetik* (*For an Ecological Aesthetics of Nature*), identified "atmosphere as the fundamental concept of a new aesthetics." Using this phrase as his title he presented the idea in lectures in 1991, and a subsequent journal article. His interest was not uniquely architecture, nor was it art proper, but rather an aesthetics that could recognize aesthetic experience wherever it occurred between subject and object—in "nature," pictures, language, advertising, or politics. Böhme credits Walter Benjamin and Hermann Schmitz as philosophical predecessors whose work helped him formulate the idea of atmospheres.

Architectural atmosphere was further explored in the final issue, in 1998, of the now defunct *Daidalos: Berlin Architectural Journal*.

With the publication of Peter Zumthor's widely read book, *Atmospheres: Architectural Environments, Surrounding Objects*, the term began to move more generally into discussions about architecture, in 2006 (the same year Gernot Böhme published his book *Arkitektur und Atmosphäre* (*Architecture and Atmosphere*).

In 2013, the Netherlands publication, *OASE Journal for Architecture*, returned to the subject with a dedicated issue featuring architectural atmosphere's chief protagonists, Gernot Böhme, Juhani Pallasmaa, and Peter Zumthor. This journal issue was especially concerned with the question of whether architectural atmosphere could be intentionally built.

In 2014, Christian Borch edited a volume, *Architectural Atmospheres: On the Experience and Politics of Architecture*, with contributions by Borch, Böhme, the artist Olafur Eliasson, and Pallasmaa. In it, Borch identifies atmospheres both as a recent trend, and approvingly, as "the atmospheric turn" (or return).

Böhme, and those who have taken up and explored the idea of atmospheres, have given those interested in architecture both a logical terminology and a precise way to talk about the experience of architecture's most significant qualities. Architectural atmosphere, in Böhme's conception, lies between object (architecture) and subject (human being). Moreover, interested as it is in a "new aesthetics" at once more egalitarian and far reaching than any aesthetics that have come before, Böhme's conception is much larger than mere architectural aesthetics. As Borch's title suggests, the concept has potentially far-reaching consequences for aesthetics.

As Böhme suggests, it is important in any discussion of atmosphere, whether in architecture or politics, to not fall sloppily back on the more casual uses of the term.

Though I am a partisan, I am suspicious of the term atmosphere because on the one hand it is the essential concept for a new aesthetics that would replace an outdated judgmental aesthetics, and on the other hand atmosphere is posited as quality in architecture, and positioned around architects just now practicing a particular aesthetic. How can it be both the thing in architecture that carries the feeling perceived by persons and the standard by which that architecture shall be judged? Böhme's warning notwithstanding, I don't entirely trust human tribes to not misuse the term atmosphere as a mark of quality. If one wishes to overthrow aesthetics because of the power it unfairly builds and wields, then it seems unwise to also make atmosphere the measure of quality in architecture. But resolving this contradiction is not simple—better to accept the value of atmospheres wherever they appear and be generous in one's appraisal of architectures wherever they are found.

Wherever you go, there you are, surrounded by atmospheres—terrible, bewildering, vile, or delightful, ennobling, loving, or proud. As Gernot Böhme points out, our casual use of the word atmosphere hovers between embarrassment and belief. We invoke the word atmosphere when we are describing something that is very nearly impossible to describe. We use the word for the very reason that it is in itself indefinable as a particular mood, even though it is entirely about moods.

It is apparent that discussion of atmospheres in architecture often involves black and white photographs. In Zumthor's *Atmospheres*, certain of the photographs that are meant to indicate what Zumthor means by atmosphere, as well as photographs meant to show the work, echo the photographs from Christopher Alexander's *The Timeless Way of Building*, that are meant to evoke and explain the "quality without a name." In *For an Architecture of Reality*, Michael Benedikt does much the same thing to demonstrate "direct aesthetic experience of the real," and the attendant attributes of the architecture he wishes to champion. In the "Building Atmosphere" issue of *OASE Journal for Architecture*, the fifteen photographs published as "Stepping Stones" similarly position atmospheres as various qualities attached to spaces. Dear reader, I suspect you can think of other examples, including some from the very book you are presently holding in your hands or beholding on a screen.

Why black and white? Is the aesthetic stance of atmosphere being built with such an appeal from the qualities of black and white photographs?

Böhme's conception of the aesthetic term atmosphere proceeds in part from the recognition that pictures can emanate atmospheres just as readily as the realities they purportedly represent, hence the usefulness of the term atmosphere for a new aesthetics generally and not only architecture specifically. So, in encountering a photograph of an architectural object or surrounding environment, one may be experiencing atmosphere in two ways—both through the picture and through the imagined content of the picture. A black and white image, being stripped of the distraction of color, and placing emphasis on light and composition, can heighten emotional qualities and above all emphasize the fact that in addition to being a scene of an actual space and place it is also a picture. Add words, as in a caption or other form of text, and the imagination of atmosphere becomes three-fold (at least for an engaged reader).

Atmosphere is something that we experience immediately, instantaneously, unconsciously, through vision (direct and peripheral) and the other senses, before we have a chance to think. Perceiving atmosphere, like perceiving faces, is egalitarian, animal, connected to survival, and built on human evolution. For architectural atmosphere, first impressions matter.

⧗

My friend Bill Huston has come to visit, and he sits at the dining room table. He looks around and appears to marvel. "It's beautiful," he says, and he says this enough, and he has this particular expression on his face, and I have known him for many years, so I know what he is saying is genuine, full of feeling. In Bill's eyes, the house is beautiful.

Once, I told a university colleague, a graphic designer, that I was designing a house for myself. She reacted immediately, saying how exciting that would be to do, but added, "That would be scary."

"What do you mean?" I asked.

"Just the pressure to get everything right."

Designing the house for myself never felt very different than designing for someone else, because when designing, I always want to make things as well as I can make them. The main difference though was the excitement of knowing that we would live in the house. What has been difficult is the knowledge that the house is one particular thing but that it could have been something else entirely. I have occasionally thought back to the discarded ideas—the courtyard house, the tower house, the different orientation on the site—and I always come rather quickly back to the strong feeling that it inevitably had to be what it is. It feels like my mind closing defensively against a threatening thought.

I know another designer would have designed the house differently, or I may have designed it differently for a different client. Many ways of designing the house would have been far worse, but perhaps one way would be better. Could I have done better?

I thought about every detail, sought to get everything right, struggled with questions, searched for parts and pieces, made choices, wanted things, vowed to not back down, compromised when I felt I had to. I weighed and considered. I drew, calculated, and positioned. I walked, looked, and decided.

It seems to me that this mental game of wondering and second-guessing has something to do with the noble desire to improve, to learn, and to do better and yet it induces madness—it's making me obsessive. It has made me obsessive, anxious, and fearful.

I think of Peter Zumthor's definition of design, and it seems a happier world in which to dwell: "associative, wild, free, ordered, and systematic thinking in images, in architectural, spatial, colorful, and sensuous pictures— this is my favorite definition of design." When I read this quote and take a step back and reflect on all that has passed in the process of designing the house I can see that what Zumthor has described is exactly what I have gone through. It is just that in the context of the quote, designing looks like a jazz riff on the saxophone (taking just moments), whereas the reality takes place over months. The essence of the definition is in the tension and contradiction among and between those dozen words: *associative, wild, free, ordered, systematic, thinking, spatial, colorful, sensuous . . . pictures*. Resolving the tensions and contradictions takes time and, if successful, the result looks effortless.

Simplicity. This seems like a difficult thing to achieve when designing. Always choose the simpler of two possible solutions. This is what I tried to do again and again all through the process. Elegance. Try to allow the design to find its own form so that it appears effortless.

One morning I wake up thinking about the floors in the house. In some places, especially upstairs, they do not lay perfectly flat, there is some cupping, and I am focused on this imperfection, feeling anxiety and regret about it. Peggy neither notices nor cares. Todd has said this might be due to the quality of the material, and also that the floors will "settle down," but I know both of these statements are untrue, designed to take away from the certainty of the real reason—that when the floors were laid there was still too much moisture in the house from the fresh framing lumber and decking and weather. Todd is also trying to insert something positive into the discussion so that over time I might continue to hope the floors will "settle down" and become gradually inured to their obvious flaw. Todd seeks to placate—I've known that. The floors, where they are cupped, are flawed—they are perhaps the most significant flaw in the house, and no amount of saying otherwise will change that. Perhaps someday I'll sand them flat again.

I think about a flaw like this and it reminds me that the house is reaching a certain state of perfection—it hasn't reached it yet—and then after that point it will begin to age, badly or well. A good building ages gracefully, and carries even its damages and shortcomings with dignity. This change will change the building's atmosphere.

⌛

The theories that operate broadly from within a phenomenological perspective serve to explain architecture as both physical objects (things) and as lived human experience (ideas, feelings)—without separating the two. That is why it is useful to bring a consideration of theories derived from phenomenology to the question of how to design, and why I have done so, even though I am wary of the fundamental inadequacy—the brute force and failing—of explanations of design. David Seamon writes:

I have come to believe strongly that phenomenology provides a useful conceptual language for bridging the environmental designer's more intuitive approach to understanding with the academic researcher's more intellectual approach. In this sense, phenomenology may be one useful way for the environment-behavior researcher to reconcile the difficult tensions between feeling and thinking and between firsthand lived experience and secondhand conceptual accounts of that experience.[8]

An environmental designer working to shape a place does not face the same task as an academic researcher but begins with a long list of considerations, the more poetic of which is how the sun will reach the building in the morning and leave it in the evening and thus initiate and conclude a series of daily activities unique to individuals but nonetheless which might be anticipated. The designer aspiring to do well will seek to make the most of their awareness and knowledge of such activities. In this series of activities the inhabitant will encounter many things besides the building proper, and the interaction with these things will at least partially involve dwelling in the sense meant by Heidegger that to build is to dwell, to dwell is to think, and to think is to make oneself at home.

Building involves not only the construct that is the building, but also the host of things (objects and details) that become a part of the identified place as well as all of the

[8] David Seamon, "Phenomenology, Place, Environment, and Architecture: A Review of the Literature," 2000. Online publication accessed June 1, 2013.http://www.arch.ksu.edu/seamon/articles/2000_phenomenology_review.htm

metaphorical and cultural connotations that attach to it with human thought and inhabitation. These things as entities that are part of the whole deserve more attention than they usually receive in architecture circles, circles that avoid concern for interiority to a surprising degree, though they are often the stuff of the practice of interior design.

In Peter Zumthor's slim volume *Atmospheres: Architectural Environments, Surrounding Objects*, first given as a talk meant to explain the renowned architect's "interests," Zumthor discusses buildings as containers for beautiful details and objects. He writes, "I'm impressed by the things that people keep around them . . . you find things come together in a very caring, loving way, and that there's this deep relationship." He believes that acquisitiveness is a part of "our true nature." He goes on to speak of how things and inhabitation go hand in hand, and together they humble him:

> The idea of things that have nothing to do with me as an architect taking their place in a building, their rightful place—it's a thought that gives me an insight into the future of my buildings: a future that happens without me. That does me a lot of good. It's a great help to me to imagine the future of rooms in a house I'm building, to imagine them actually in use.[9]

Acknowledgements such as this one, of the significance of interior objects, are rare among architects. It is far more common to hear disparagement of an owner's ugly intrusions upon a design. This habit is also connected with Modernism

---

[9] Peter Zumthor, *Atmospheres: Architectural Environments, Surrounding Objects*, (Basel, Switzerland, Birkhäuser, 2006), p. 35.

as a minimalistic style in which the designer plans for every contingency and thereby achieves not only a machine for living but also a spare, relatively object-free environment, or a total work of art. Where interior objects do constitute an intentional element of design there is an understandable desire for sole authorship and control. But what is overlooked in this perspective is the intimate connections between people and things that shape the intimate connections between people and places.

I designed my house to feel in contrast to but continuous with the surrounding forest. This was accomplished largely, though not completely, through the extent of the openings between inside and outside. The goal, rather than a total work of art, was a world of objects of diverse sources. Specific objects in the interior blur the boundaries between the surrounding natural world, building, building craft, crafts as furnishing, and art. In terms of aesthetic experience, the result in the house, I believe, is a smooth continuum from nature to culture. In their differences, materials and objects play across aesthetic categories, satisfying in an actual sense the Deweyan principle of art as experience. Materials and objects quietly move and stimulate, not needing to be perfectly consistent with each other, recovering, as Dewey wished, the continuity of aesthetic experience within ordinary processes of living. Or at least that is what I say now that the building has taken place.

⌛

One day I go for a walk in the woods. There is a preserve near the house with a trail that goes down to the shore and returns in a big loop. I usually go left when I enter and walk in a clockwise direction, so when I reach the cove I am walking more or less from east to west. On this particular morning I go the other way around because the last few days I have been walking mindlessly. I have been in a bit of a rut.

I have also been thinking I would like to go driftwood hunting. The idea seems slightly stupid—to make a special trip to look for pieces of wood that happen to wash up on the shore. It feels absurd for intention to go in search of accident. Still, I recall a wonderful day on the porch of a rental house painting driftwood with Callie and Hugh, and I miss them, and perhaps we could do it again when they return. I might increase the chance of finding driftwood by driving to Oak Point, where the ocean washes in from both sides, where there is a beach on each side of the road. But I am walking now; I can look for driftwood now on the rocks on this morning's walk.

I am still walking mindlessly, vigorously, and not concentrating. I realize minutes have gone by without awareness, and I hate that sensation. I can't see very well, either, because I am wearing my dark sunglasses with the distance lenses that tend to make seeing very clearly at my feet slightly uncomfortable.

In ten minutes I am near the shore. I take a short side path and break out into the blazing light, and the sparkling glare of low tide, looking east into the sun. I listen to the gentle hiss of seaweed as it settles in among rocks. Scanning the rocks I can see almost at once that there is no driftwood to be found. I look around a few moments more then return to the trail the same way I came.

On the trail I walk a few paces then stop. There is a small piece of driftwood in the path and I pick it up. It is roughly square, but it has been at sea a very long time. It is beautiful and interesting and I wonder if someone has dropped it there. Why else would it be in the path? I walk a few more paces, then stop. A spruce trunk, tipped halfway over, its disk of roots pulled up into the air, blocks the way, and beyond it lays another blowdown, much larger and spiked with branches. The path is completely blocked, which surprises me, since the weather has been calm and I came this way yesterday and the day before that.

So to get around the blowdown I turn back and return to the beach, out into the sunlight again, and I walk along through the damp grasses and gravel looking for the overturned roots and the blowdown and when I see the roots I stop to study them, expecting to see that the overturn is fresh but it is not. There is what looks like a flurry of seagull droppings, but it is congealed spruce sap, and there are other signs that the tree fell some time ago. Why was the path not blocked yesterday?

I look closely at the shore for an opening where I might climb up into the woods and onto the path again, past the blowdown. I find a faint path, and discover in the grasses a trove of driftwood pieces. There is one board a yard long that I like, and four or five others. I make a stack of them and, happy with my discoveries, push through to the path again. On the path I walk back, out of curiosity, in the direction of the blowdown but I do not find it, which is surprising and strange. I decide it must now be quite far back along the path, so I turn around again.

Walking now, I have the worrying feeling that I do not recognize the path. I know from long experience that a walking path experienced in one direction can feel entirely different when walked in the other direction, unless there are some very distinct landmarks. I try to use this knowledge to reassure myself, but the more I walk the stranger the woods feel. I am also troubled by the thought of the impasse behind me. Why did I not reach the blowdown when I walked back toward it? Was I somehow now on a different trail? The thought is unsettling to me: I've walked here enough to know that there is but one trail.

I stop, lay down the pile of driftwood, and turn around. I walk a hundred paces, much farther than I believe should be necessary to reach the blowdown, but still the trail is open, and my mind races to cover all the possible explanations. Come back tomorrow and walk in the usual direction, I say to myself, perhaps then it will be clear.

I turn around again and walk in the direction of the road and home and I half expect to discover that the pile of driftwood has disappeared, but in a few paces there it is. I pick it up, at least partially relieved, and walk onward, but the trail continues to feel unfamiliar for a long way. I wonder again if I have somehow stumbled onto an unknown side trail, but before long I come to a distinct bend in the trail that I know. From this point onward I relax and walk and think about what a strange experience I have had, how the woods feel like a wilderness and the path a perplexing universe. The experience has reminded me of my first days camping on the land, when I listened in the night with hyper-vigilance, received every sense impression in a heightened state of attention, and sought to make sense of chaos.

At the end of the path I walk out into the small gravel parking lot, cross it, and turn left onto the road. I readjust the pile of driftwood because my hand feels numb and stiff. It is a nice little pile of driftwood. I will enjoy painting these pieces with Callie and Hugh when they come home.

At the place in the road where the sunlight pours in, where the trees are cut through down to the shore, there is a big yellow house—a nineteenth-century clapboard four-square with white trim. There is an old Volvo wagon with a roof rack there, parked way back on the scant drive, and I wonder for a moment if the people in the house come often, if they are renters, or if they own the house. It is a modest and simple house, though large, and perhaps they know the house well, have come here often and for many years. I hear the clattering of dishes. The windows are all open. It is such a fine, bright morning. I hear the voice of a man and then the voice of a girl in response, and the dish sound again, and I suddenly think of my own house, just a five minute walk away, and I feel a surge of elation, of joy, and words suddenly form and I think how happy I am to have a house without history.

On that day, sitting at the table and then out walking, having taken delight in my house without history, dumbfounded by my inability to see it, the house was finished. All the work was over and yet hardly any memory had been built up. There was no significant store of memory yet to recall. For me, the place called "the house" was still more or less a blank slate

Writing, which begins with the blank page, is itself a kind of architectural process. Living there going on six summers now, on the page and in actuality, I've built memory, which is itself the mirror of imagination.

After that day I went on to design and build the garden shed, to site and design and build a fence for the garden, and to daydream into being a second small house and a workshop. I even worked the plan out on paper, imagining two large black cubes in close proximity to one another, a house meant to be retreated into in winter. I imagined the two black cubes in a flat clearing surrounded by oaks about halfway down the road. I don't know if I'll ever build this winter house and workshop, but it's fun to think about.

Sources

Christopher Alexander, *A Pattern Language: Towns, Buildings, Construction,* (New York: Oxford University Press, 1977).

Christopher Alexander, *The Timeless Way of Building,* (New York: Oxford University Press, 1979).

Gaston Bachelard, *The Poetics of Space,* (Boston: Beacon Press, 1969).

Michael Benedikt, *For an Architecture of Reality,* (New York: Lumen Books, 1987).

Gernot Böhme, "Atmosphere as the Fundamental Concept of a New Aesthetics," (Boston, MA: MIT Press), *Thesis Eleven,* Number 36, pp. 113-126.

Gernot Böhme, *The Aesthetics of Atmospheres,* ed. Jean-Paul Thibaud (London: Routledge, 2017).

Christian Borch, ed. *Architectural Atmospheres: On the Experience and Politics of Architecture,* (Basel: Birkhauser, 2015).

Ann Cline, *A Hut of One's Own: Life Outside the Circle of Architecture,* (Cambridge, MA, MIT Press, 1997).

John Dewey, *Art as Experience,* (New York: Capricorn, 1934).

Marco Frascari, *Eleven Exercises in the Art of Architectural Drawing: Slow Food for the Architect's Imagination*, (New York: Routledge, 2011).

Edward Ford, *The Architectural Detail*, (New York: Princeton Architectural Press, 2011). Edward Ford, *Five Houses, Ten Details*, (New York: Princeton Architectural Press, 2009).

Edward Ford, *The Details of Modern Architecture*, vols.1 & 2 (Cambridge, MA: MIT Press, 1990).

Tonino Griffero, tr. Sarah de Sanctis, *Atmospheres: Aesthetics of Emotional Spaces*, (Surrey: UK, Ashgate, 2014).

Larry Haun, *A Carpenter's Life as Told by Houses*, (Newtown, CT: Taunton Press, 2011).

Bill Henderson, *Tower: Faith, Vertigo, and Amateur Construction*, (New York: Farrar, Straus and Giroux, 2000).

Ben Jacks, "Reimagining Walking: Four Practices," *Journal of Architectural Education*, (Boston, MA: MIT Press), 57:3, February, 2004, 5-9.

Ben Jacks, "Walking and Reading in Landscape," *Landscape Journal*, (Madison, WI: University of Wisconsin Press), 26:2, September, 2007.

Louis I. Kahn, "The Room, the Street, and Human Agreement," talk given on the occasion of the awarding of the Gold Medal of the American Institute of Architects, 1971. AIA Journal, vol. 56, no. 3, September, 1971, pp. 33-34.

Tracy Kidder, *House*, (New York: Houghton Mifflin, 1985).

Charles Moore, Gerald Allen, and Donlyn Lyndon, *The Place of Houses*, (New York: Holt, Rhinehart, and Winston, 1974).

Christian Norberg-Schulz, *Genius Loci: Towards a Phenomenology of Architecture*, (New York: Rizzoli, 1980).

Christian Norberg-Schulz, *Existence, Space, and Architecture*, (New York: Praeger, 1971).

Juhani Pallasmaa, *The Eyes of the Skin,* (Chichester, UK: Wiley, 2005).

Juhani Pallasmaa, *The Thinking Hand: Existential and Embodied Wisdom in Architecture,* (Chicester, UK: Wiley, 2009).

Michael Pollan, *A Place of My Own: the Education of an Amateur Builder,* (New York: Random House, 1997).

David Pye, *The Nature and Art of Workmanship*, (London: Cambridge University Press: 1968).

Witold Rybczynski, *The Most Beautiful House in the World,* (New York: Peguin, 1989).

Bernard Rudofsky, *Architecture Without Architects: a Short Introduction to Non-pedigreed Architecture,* (New York: Doubleday, 1964).

Simon Unwin, *Analysing Architecture,* (New York: Routledge, 2014).

Emmanuel Viollet-le-Duc, *How to Build a House: an Architectural Novelette,* translated by Benjamin Bucknall, (London: Sampson Low,1876).

Peter Zumthor, *Atmospheres: Architectural Environments, Surrounding Objects* (Basel, Birkhäuser, 2006).

Acknowledgements

First of all, I would like to thank those who built the house, ably led by Todd Lawson of Lawson Builders: Bob Campbell, Jim Cust, David Eaton, Tony Eaton, Mike Flanders, Curt Haskell, Clay Haskell, Lars Johnson, Anna Lawson, Sarah Lawson, Todd Lawson, Scott Parker, Brian Patterson, Jason Riley, Walter Smith, Tristan Soloman, Joey Tardiff, Bill Turner, and Hank Whitsett. There are others who worked on the house whose names are unknown to me, but whose fine work still speaks. Thank you.

Thanks also to Bill Huston, Saer Huston, and Huston & Company.

Thanks to Danny Weed, for educating me about trees and how to thin a forest for optimum health, and to Farrell Rupert for doing the high and heavy work. Thanks also to Lance Hallock for digging, and lifting heavy things, honestly and with care.

Thank you to Bruce Bulger and Holley Mead, who tolerated our intrusion, and graciously welcomed us home.

Thanks to the Schrag family for permission to publish "Red Sun-Dark Woods," by Karl Schrag, and to The Turtle Gallery, Deer Isle, for providing the photograph.

Thanks to Juan Restrepo and Madison Scheper for help with illustrations, and to John Humphries for generating the shear wall studies.

Barbara Hurd, Baron Wormser, Debra Marquart, and Richard Hoffman—teachers at Stonecoast—your able eyes, ears, and pens still guide.

And thanks to Annie Finch and Glen Brand, for whom this book waited.

To three anonymous readers, whose honest appraisal and critique contributed greatly to the manuscript, thanks—it changed for the better because of you.

Thank you also, my dear colleagues, Murali Paranandi, for genuine friendship, and Gülen Çevik—your integrity and humor make everything ok.

Finally, thanks to Peggy Shaffer, for her constant love, support, and encouragement, and to our children, Callie and Hugh, who are the true inspiration.

About the Author

Ben Jacks holds degrees from the University of Chicago, the University of Pennsylvania, and the Stonecoast MFA Program in Creative Writing at the University of Southern Maine. He is a licensed architect and teaches at Miami University, Oxford, Ohio.

He is the author of *The Architect's Tour: Notes for the Design Traveler* (Culicidae Architectural Press, 2015), a book based on a year spent teaching, traveling, and taking photographs in Europe. His scholarly writing has been published in *Journal of Architectural Education*, *Places*, and *Landscape Journal*.

As a designer, Ben focuses on detail and craft, seeking to develop the potentially rich and intimate relationship between landscape, building, dwelling, and interior.

In 1991 Ben walked the Appalachian Trail, 2000 miles from Georgia to his home in Maine, and that made all the difference.

www.ingramcontent.com/pod-product-compliance
Lightning Source LLC
Chambersburg PA
CBHW060047100426
42742CB00014B/2731